MILI

This Armada book belongs to:

Alison Prince hated school. "It was so boring," she says. "I spent most of the time dreaming up adventures—which never happened, of course. That's why it's been such fun to write stories about Mill Green, where they really do happen."

As well as writing, Alison Prince has worked in television and at the Zoo (serving teas at the Penguin Bar), has sold newspapers, gilded picture frames, run a smallholding (getting up at dawn to milk the cows), driven a cattle truck, painted scenery, made furniture and hitchhiked across most of Europe. She wrote and illustrated *The Good Pets Guide* for Armada and is also responsible for the delightful drawings in Armada's *Hello to Ponies* and *Hello to Riding* by Jane Allen and Mary Danby.

At present Alison Prince lives in a cottage in Lincolnshire "about the size of a teacosy", and has no idea what will happen next. That, she says, is what keeps life interesting.

Also in Armada

Mill Green on Fire

More stories about Mill Green will be published in Armada

ALISON PRINCE

Mill Green on Stage

An Armada Original

Mill Green on Stage was first published in the U.K.
in 1982 in Armada by Fontana Paperbacks,
14 St James's Place, London SW1A 1PS.

Printed in Great Britain by
Love & Malcomson Ltd., Brighton Road,
Redhill, Surrey.

Contents

To Lucy and Mischa, who were very helpful

CHAPTER 1

The Newcomer

It was morning break at Mill Green School, and Matt, Danny, Sue and Rachel were sitting on a bench outside, eating crisps. Although it was October, the sun shone brightly and it was nicer out here on the paved area with its shrubs and benches than in a classroom. Mill Green had been built to look more like a collection of barns than a conventional school, and its dark timbers and sloping roofs made the areas between the buildings seem rather like farm-yards.

"Hey!" said Danny suddenly. "Look at that!" A long, gleaming black car drew into the bus park in front of Mr Hazzard's office and stopped.

Matt glanced up from under the fair hair which always flopped forward into his eyes. "It's a Rolls," he said.

"'Spect we're being visited by the Mayor or something," said Rachel. She finished her last crisp, crumpled up the bag and aimed it at the red-painted litter bin.

"Missed," said Matt. He looked at the huge car again and added, "Well, it certainly isn't the Mayor."

A man wearing jeans and a rather dirty donkey jacket had got out of the driving seat. He went round to the passenger door, opened it, and helped out a girl with amazingly bright red hair. She wore tight black trousers, high-heeled shoes with ankle straps, and a denim battledress top.

"And *she's* not the Mayoress," agreed Rachel. "She's only about the same age as us."

"My mum would murder me if I went out looking like that," said plump little Sue Eames. "Look, she's got great big dangly earrings, too. And I bet her hair's not really that colour."

"Looks like shredded beetroot," said Danny.

They watched, fascinated, as the man handed the girl a bright orange canvas bag with pockets and straps all over it. He shut the car door and locked it, then he and the girl came towards the school.

"They're going to the Head's offfice," said Danny.

"You don't suppose she's coming here, do you?" asked Rachel excitedly. "I do hope she is!"

"I don't," said Sue. "I think she looks awful. All posh and snooty."

"Exactly," agreed Rachel gleefully. "She'll be wonderfully teasable. I can't wait!"

"Mr Hazzard wouldn't have a girl like that in our school," said Danny smugly. "He told Felicity not to wear that ring her mother gave her. And that was on her *birthday*."

"You can talk!" said Sue, laughing. "You look like a walking scarecrow, Danny!"

"I *small* walking scarecrow," corrected Matt.

"I can't help it," said Danny, unrepentant. "Mum doesn't like sewing buttons on."

"That's no reason for wearing odd socks," said Sue.

Danny looked down at his feet, clad in grubby plimsolls, one grey sock and one blue one. "Oh," he said, without much surprise. "So they are."

The bell went and everyone drifted back into the building, reluctant to leave the autumn sunshine.

Matt picked up Rachel's crisps bag and threw it in the bin. "It's a funny time to start in a new school, isn't it?" he said. "In the middle of the term. If she *is* coming here, that is."

"Funny time of the day, too," said Rachel. "Why couldn't she turn up at quarter to nine, same as the rest of us?"

"Perhaps she was still snuggled between her silken sheets," said Sue rather dreamily, "waiting for her maid to bring breakfast on a tray."

"Oh, yuk," said Rachel.

The next lesson was English.

"Settle down!" said Mr Potter loudly. "What's all the gabble about this morning? Has a spacecraft landed in the bus park or something?"

"No, a Rolls Royce," said Rachel, grinning. "I was just telling Felicity about it—"

"And I was telling Deb," said Sue.

"Oh, for goodness' sake!" Mr Potter ran his fingers through his hair crossly. "We must get *started*. You don't need any textbooks today, just your English notebooks and a pen."

"Left my pen at home, sir," said Peter Box.

"Incompetent twit," said Mr Potter. "Borrow one when we start writing—*without fuss*. Now, everyone quiet."

When all the shuffling and chattering had stopped, Mr Potter went on: "One of the chief reasons why we try to teach you English at school is so that you can use words to say exactly what you mean." Warming to his subject, he continued, "Look how many people these days can't string two words together—even about something they know like the back of their hands. Ask them what sort of house they live in, and what do you get?" He put on the expression of somebody extremely stupid. "'Er—well—it's like—er—a house, innit?'"

"What's the matter with that?" asked John Beasley.

"What's the *matter* with it?" roared Mr Potter. "*Everythings's* the matter with it. It's dull, inarticulate and totally lacking in information. It's—"

The door opened and Mr Hazzard came in, followed by the girl who had got out of the Rolls Royce. She dumped her large orange bag on the nearest desk, which happened to belong to Bill North, and put one hand on her hip as though she felt unutterably bored. She gave a faint yawn and studied her scarlet-varnished fingernails.

"Sorry to interrupt your lesson, Mr Potter," said the Headmaster. "We have a new pupil this morning and I've allocated her to your group, at least for the time being, until we've completed the assessment tests." He lowered his voice and added, "I have already mentioned the earrings and the nail varnish. And I'd be glad if you could spare me a moment at ten past twelve."

"He's going to tell Mr Potter all about her," Danny whispered to Matt, who nodded agreement.

Mr Hazzard turned his attention to the class. "I do hope

you people will show your usual courtesy towards our newcomer," he said. "Her name is Marcia Mudd and—"

An outburst of snorts and giggles interrupted him, but he glared at the offenders angrily until quiet was restored. In the moment's pause, Marcia looked up from her nails and said, "S'what you expect, innit?" She gave the glass a contemptuous stare and added, "Pigs!". Then she returned to inspecting her nails.

"Phew!" said Rachel, shaking her fingers as if they were hot. "Nice!"

"You can get your blooming bag off my desk," said Bill North. Marcia removed it and turned it over to brush the bottom of it carefully with her hand, as though it might have been contaminated.

"I'm sure you'll all settle down very soon if people just remember their manners," said Mr Hazzard with a steely glint behind his spectacles. "Now, where is there an empty desk? This one beside you will do, Bill."

"I'm not sitting next to *him*," said Marcia, clutching her bag in both arms like a mother protecting her child.

"Sit beside Felicity," said Mr Potter. "Over by the window, look."

Marcia made her way distastefully between the rows of desks and floppped down beside Felicity without looking at her.

"Right," said Mr Hazzard, smiling affably. "I'll leave you to it. See you later, Mr Potter."

"Ten past twelve," Mr Potter promised.

Mr Hazzard headed towards the door and was momentarily entangled with Stephen Chuff, who decided at the last moment to open the door for the Headmaster but succeeded only in colliding with him.

Rachel shook her head, laughing. "Isn't he lovely!" she said.

"Who, Stephen?" enquired Matt.

"No, Mr Hazzard, you idiot! He's so tall, and that wispy beard and everything."

"Daft, you are," said Matt.

"Now, then," said Mr Potter firmly as Stephen returned to his seat. "Let's get on. Where had I got to?"

"Houses," said Debbie Smart.

"Yes. Marcia, you haven't missed anything, actually. I was just saying how important it is to be able to use words to make people understand exactly what you are talking about. If you want to describe your house, the idea is to make someone who's never seen it understand what sort of place you live in. Now, think about it. What are some of the words that spring to mind when you imagine a house?"

"Telly," said John Beasley.

"No," said Mr Potter firmly. "A TV set can be anywhere. Hospital, airport lounge—anywhere. Think again Try some describing words. Small, large . . .?"

"Clean," said Rachel primly.

"Cosy?" suggested Sue.

"Warm," said Matt.

"Yes," agreed Mr Potter, "but it's always the same people all the time. I want *all* of you to think. In a minute I'm going to ask you to write a description of your own house, trying to make it so real that if I came there I'd feel as if I already knew it."

Marcia stared at him from under the strands of plum-red hair which hung over her dark eyebrows. "You don't go to people's houses, do you?" she demanded.

"No, of course not," said Mr Potter. "Not unless I'm invited. No, we're talking about writing good, clear English, that's all. Now, what I suggest you do is start at your bedroom and describe what that's like. Put in all the little details that nobody else would know. Then say what's outside your bedroom door and talk about the bathroom perhaps, and say what other rooms there are. Then come down the stairs, as it were, noticing things like the banisters and what colour the wall is, and the stair carpet."

"Then do the sitting room and dining room and kitchen?" suggested Rachel.

"Quite," said Mr Potter. "And, Rachel, do remember kitchen has got a T in it. Try thinking of making Tea in the *kit*chen."

"Isn't that clever!" said Rachel admiringly. "No wonder you're a teacher, sir!"

"Flattery will get you everywhere," said Mr Potter. "Any questions before you start?"

"What about the garden?" asked Stephen Chuff. "And if you've got outbuildings and things?"

"Put them in if you've got time," said Mr Potter.

"All you've got to do with *your* house," Matt said to Stephen, "is describe the goats and the pigsties and the barley field. Nobody would need any more."

"Don't start chatting among yourselves," said Mr Potter. "Open your notebooks and put the heading, 'My House'." He wrote it on the blackboard behind him. "And today's date is October the fourteenth." He turned round again, dusting his hands, and noticed Marcia, who had not moved from where she sat, still clutching her bag on her lap. He made his way betwen the desks towards her.

"Now, Marcia," he said cheerfully, "I don't expect you've got a notebook, have you?"

Marcia seemed to think the answer to this question was obvious and made no reply.

"What school did you go to before you came here?" Mr Potter enquired.

"Manor Vale, last one," said Marcia.

"And where was that?" asked Mr Potter.

"London."

"Whereabouts in London? It's a big place."

Marcia sighed. "Hackney."

"Oh, yes. And were you there long?"

"Long enough," said Marcia.

"You could put your bag on the floor, you know," suggested Mr Potter.

"No, thanks."

It was Mr Potter's turn to sigh. "You're not going to be able to write with a great big bag on your lap," he pointed out.

"Can't write without a book, can I?" Marcia retorted.

"I'll get you one," said Mr Potter, retreating.

Felicity underlined her title neatly, then, seeing Mr Potter rootling in the cupboard for a notebook, turned to her new neighbour and said, "You don't have to be stroppy with Mr Potter. He's all right. He really tries to be nice."

"That's what they all say," said Marcia.

Mr Potter came back with a new notebook. "Put your name on the cover," he said. "No need to leave any spaces to catch up work—what you've missed, you've missed. Not your fault.Start on the first page and rule a margin."

With one hand, Marcia opened the book and creased its cover back. She dug in her bag and produced a ballpoint pen and, leaning across the top of the bag, began to write in a rapid, contemptuous way. She did not draw a margin.

Mr Potter went from desk to desk, reading what people had written and offering advice. Marcia had completed several pages by the time he reached her, and she sat back reluctantly to let him pick up her book and read what she had written.

"I say!" he remarked when he had finished. "You do live in a splendid house! It sounds absolutely marvellous."

Marcia shrugged.

"You write very fluently," Mr Potter added, "but you tend to run on a bit. There are lots of places where you could do with a full stop or two. Like here—'The bathroom is quite decent it has gold taps the bath is the sort you step down into there is a palm tree in a marble pot.' You need to break it up a bit. After 'gold taps' you need a full stop, and another before you say, 'there is a palm tree'. See what I mean?"

"Yeah," said Marcia.

"And rule a margin," added Mr Potter. Then he went back to his desk, glancing at his watch. "Bell will go in a minute," he said. "Anyone finished?"

Two or three hands went up, Rachel's among them.

"Rachel, you'd better check yours with a dictionary," said Mr Potter. "Try and do something about the spelling before I see it and have my usual fit. Anyone else who's finished, read it through carefully for silly mistakes—the rest of you, finish it. That's your homework."

Sue groaned. "I thought you'd forgotten, sir," she said.

"I'm not just a pretty face, you know," said Mr Potter grimly. The bell went and everyone stood up, stuffing books into their bags although, since this was their form room, there was no hurry to go anywhere else.

"Marcia, do you know where the canteen is?" asked Mr Potter above the babble of conversation.

Marcia nodded. "I can smell it," she said. "Makes you sick. Think I'll go out."

"You're not allowed to go out," said Mr Potter. "You can't leave the premises without a note from your parents. Have you got some dinner money?"

Marcia gave him a withering look. "'*Course* I got money," she said. Then she shouldered the orange bag and walked out.

Mr Potter pushed his books and papers into his battered briefcase and hurried away, glancing at his watch again.

"I'd love to know what Mr Hazzard is going to tell him about our Marcia," said Rachel. "Isn't she *awful*!"

"I thought she'd be really posh," said Danny. "Arriving in a Rolls and everything. But she isn't, is she?"

"Gives herself airs, though," put in Debbie. "Did you hear that bit Mr Potter read out about the gold taps?"

"Gold taps, my foot," said Rachel. "I don't believe a word of it."

"But she couldn't have made it up," said Felicity, joining in the conversation. "And why not gold taps, anyway? If they've got a Rolls Royce they must have heaps of money."

"I suppose rich people don't always *look* rich," mused Sue. "We went to a stately home once when I was small, and my dad got talking to a shabby old chap who was pruning a rosebush. They went on for ages about gardens and then it turned out the old chap was His Lordship. He owned this huge house and everything. My mum was ever so embarrassed."

"Why?" asked Rachel. "Having money doesn't make one person better than another. It's more like a kind of sport, really, seeing how much you can make."

"I wonder where Marcia lives," said Matt. "Mum and I only moved here last year, and it's not much fun at first when you don't know anyone. We ought to try and be friendly, really."

"You're such a *good* boy, Matt," said Rachel. "I don't know why I'm friends with you, really. Come on—let's go and get some dinner before all the chips go. I hate mash."

They went out of the classroom and along the corridor towards the canteen.

"When my brother was here they had old-fashioned school dinners," said Stephen. "Meat and two veg and gravy. And puds with custard."

"I like puds with custard," said Danny.

Matt looked down at his small friend and said, "That's because you're trying to grow."

"Puds only make you grow outwards," said Sue mournfully. "That's why I don't eat them."

"I don't know why you fuss about it," said Rachel. "You're not really *fat*, anyway. If I were you I'd eat lots of whatever I liked and be a *huge* lady. And wear wonderful traily clothes with fringes and dangly bits. Velvet and tassels."

"And what would Mr Potter say if I arrived in velvet and tassels?" demanded Sue hotly. "Don't be such a twit, Rachel."

Rachel tossed her curly head. "It's all very well for you," she said. "You've got curves. I look like one of those desk lamps made of long, skinny steel bits, with little springs in the hinges." To illustrate what she meant, she walked like a desk lamp, shooting out her arms and legs abruptly and making clicking noises.

"Mind!" shrieked Sue. They had entered the wide part of the corridor where the dining tables were, and Rachel's flailing arms had narrowly missed Mrs Abbott, on her way to join some other teachers with a laden tray.

"Rachel!" thundered Mrs Abbott. "*What* are you doing?"

"Sorry, Mrs Abbott," said Rachel meekly. "I was being a desk lamp."

"*Stupid* girl," said Mrs Abbott. "Get along at once and try to behave yourself."

Rachel dropped a tiny curtsey, looking even sillier, and scuttled on. "I hope your omelette's tough," she muttered.

"I hate Mrs Abbott," said Sue loyally. "She never thinks anything's funny."

"She can't help it," said Rachel as they joined the queue for the service hatch. "She's just a handicapped person"

"What d'you mean?" asked Danny.

"Well, she's got something missing, hasn't she?" said Rachel. "She doesn't work properly. Things that make other people laugh just make her cross. Poor old thing."

"Look," said Felicity. "There's the Queen of Sheba."

Some distance away, Marcia sat with a plate of chips before her, which she was eating with her fingers.

"Naice manners they 'ave at the 'All, don't they?" said Stephen.

"Let's go and join her," said Sue. "Look, there's plenty of room at her table."

"Go and bag the seats," said Rachel. "I'll get your dinner for you. What do you want, dreary old cheese salad?"

"Yes, please," said Sue. "And a pot of yoghurt. A pink one."

"Pink's fattening!" Rachel called after her, but Sue pretended not to hear.

"Oh, good, there's steak and kidney pud as well as chips," said Rachel, rubbing her hands with glee. "A nice dinner *and* Marcia Mudd! I'm looking forward to this!"

CHAPTER 2

The Pantomime

Sue dumped herself down opposite Marcia and smiled. "Hello," she said. Marcia glanced at her coolly and went on eating chips.

"I said, 'hello'," repeated Sue, nettled.

Marcia sighed. Unhurriedly, she finished the chip she was eating and said, "Hello." Then she ate another chip.

Sue felt inclined to ask the new girl why she was so rude but, as she stared at the unnatural red hair and the thin-lipped, contemptuous mouth, she lost her nerve. This girl would win any verbal battle hands down. Sue went on staring and Marcia shot her a sudden, hostile glance from her darkly made-up eyes.

"Wotcher staring at?" she demanded.

"Nothing," said Sue, confused. "I just—thought your earrings were pretty, that's all."

"Oh, did you?" Marcia fingered the dangling gypsy rings. "Gold, they are."

"Yes, I thought they were," said Sue meekly.

Marcia finished her last chip, fished in a pocket of her orange bag and brought out a clean, folded handkerchief with lace edges. She shook it out and wiped her fingers on it. Then she pushed it back in her bag and looked up at Sue mockingly. "How would you know?" she asked.

Sue blushed. "Know what?"

"If they was gold or not. You wouldn't know chalk from cheese, would you? Never been out of this little hole of a town you live in, have you?"

"I've been to London," Sue protested. "Twice."

"Oh, yeah? Feed the pigeons in Trafalgar Square, did you?"

"Well, yes," admitted Sue. "And then we went to a theatre."

Marcia slumped back in her chair. "Don't make me laugh," she said.

Sue looked up in relief as Rachel approached with a piled-high tray. "Here we are," she said, sliding the tray on to the table. "Big dinner for me, little one for you."

"Thanks," said Sue. "How much was mine."

"Doesn't matter," said Rachel airily, "any time'll do." Sue looked at her in some surprise. Rachel was not usually so casual about money. Perhaps she wanted to show Marcia that she, too, took it completely for granted. Rachel unloaded the plates quickly, put the tray on the stand with the others and sat down beside Sue as Matt and Danny and the others came to join them.

"Well," said Rachel brightly, glancing from Marcia to Sue. "And how are we getting on, then? Found a new friend, Sue?"

Sue cut a lettuce leaf in half and said crossly, "Pass the salt."

"Don't be huffy," said Rachel. "I was only joking." She took a large mouthful of steak and kidney pudding and added, "M'm—lovely!"

Matt, who was sitting beside Marcia, said, "Where do you live?"

"Big place out in the country," said Marcia dismissively. "Don't suppose they let you smoke in here, do they?"

"No, of course they don't," said Matt.

"Smoking is disgusting," said Rachel.

Marcia ignored her. "Have to go in the loo, then," she said. "All the same, these bloody schools."

"No, don't rush off," said Matt. "We're only trying to be friendly."

"I'm not," said Rachel cheerfully.

This was too much to ignore. "What's the matter with you then?" Marcia asked her. "Jealous?"

"*Jealous?*" Rachel pretended to choke over her dinner. "What of?"

"Bet your dad ain't got a Roller," said Marcia.

"A what?" asked Danny.

"A Roller. Rolls Royce to you, sunshine."

"Nobody needs a car that size," said Rachel firmly. "It's very antisocial, having a car that uses so much petrol."

"Get off," said Marcia scornfully. "You'd like one, same as everyone else."

Rachel went on eating her dinner unhurriedly. Then she said, "Whereabouts is this place in the country you're supposed to live in?"

Marcia looked at her through narrowed eyes with intense dislike. "Mind your own business!" she retorted.

"Don't be so rude!" Felicity said indignantly.

"I don't have to tell people where I live," said Marcia. "I'm fussy, I am. My dad don't want all sorts of riff-raff poking round our place."

Rachel lost her temper. "Look here, you snotty old bag," she said. "I don't care *what* sort of place you live in. I wouldn't care if your mother was the Queen of England. As far as I'm concerned, people are either nice or they're not. And you're not."

"She might be when you get to know her," said Sue bravely.

"Oh, might she?" Rachel turned on her friend in astonishment. "And whose side are *you* on?"

"I'm not on anyone's side," muttered Sue, crimson-faced "I just think we don't know her very well, that's all."

"You don't have to stick up for me, bun-face," said Marcia. "I don't need no help." She nodded at Rachel and added, "I should pay Little Miss Smarty-pants for your dinner if I were you, before she sends the 'eavies round to get the money."

Rachel half rose to her feet, fists clenched. "You utter—*bitch*!" she said.

"Not a very peaceful dinner time, is it?" said Danny.

Marcia stood up. "Don't worry," she said. "I'm going. Pull your chairs in so's I can get out. They pack you in like cattle in this place."

"Say please," put in Stephen from Danny's other side.

Marcia glared at him. "You better let me out," she said,

"or I'll walk across the table." And she put one high-heeled foot on her chair.

"She means it," said Matt gloomily. The boys pulled their chairs in tight to the table, and Marcia squeezed past behind them, her orange bag scraping their shoulders.

"Now say thank you!" Stephen called after her as Marcia stalked away across the dining area. She did not look back, but held up two fingers in a gesture which caused eyebrows to be raised on the staff table.

"Ooh! said Rachel through clenched teeth. "I *hate* her!"

"Really?" said Danny innocently. "You don't think she's lovely, then? Not like Mr Hazzard and Mr Potter and—"

"Oh, shut up," said Rachel.

"Tell you what," said Matt, who had been thinking. "The register has all our addresses in it, beside our names. And I take it down to the office twice a day. I'll soon find out where her country house is."

"Oh, yes!" said Rachel with dawning pleasure. "What a good idea, Matt! And once we know, we'll have another session with Madam."

"I'd rather not," said Sue, scooping up the last of her yoghurt.

Rachel regarded her friend thoughtfully. "You know what's the matter with you, don't you?" she said. "You're afraid of her."

"No, I'm not!" protested Sue. But the tell-tale blush crept across her face again and she secretly feared that Rachel was right.

"What on earth have we here?" said Mr Watts, staring at Marcia in disbelief. Everyone giggled. Marcia folded her arms and stared back. "I have learned from hard experience," Mr Watts went on, tight-lipped, "that people like you are apt to have hypersensitive parents who utter screams of protest if their little darlings are told what they look like. I *could* tell you what you look like but consideration for the more decent girls in the class prevents me from doing so. You will *not* in future attend this school wearing nail varnish or what appear to be Christmas tree baubles dangling from your ears."

"Yeah, I know," said Marcia. "He said."

"*Who* said?"

"The other bloke. The 'ead."

"Mr Hazzard," corrected Mr Watts. "Good. Perhaps there is some faint chance that you will look slightly more presentable tomorrow. What Maths have you done?"

"Not a lot," said Marcia.

"Have you been using these SMP books?" persisted Mr Watts, holding up a textbook.

"Yeah," said Marcia. "Think so."

"Not 'yeah'," insisted Mr Watts furiously. "Say, 'yes, sir'."

"Yesss—*sir*," said Marcia with contempt.

"Which book were you on most recently?"

"Dunno. C, I think."

Mr Watts sighed. "You'd better start with the others and see how you get on. You know what decimals are, do you?"

"Yeah," said Marcia. "Little dot, innit? Numbers both sides of it."

Mr Watts closed his eyes despairingly for a moment, placing the fingertips of one hand on his bald forehead. When he looked at her again, Marcia showed no trace of a smile, although the rest of the class was in fits of laughter. "That'll do!" he snapped. "You can start with the revision exercise, multiplication and division of decimals. Everybody should get these right. There is no excuse for any mistakes."

"May I have a book, please. *Sir*," said Marcia.

"That's better," said Mr Watts. But this time, as he turned away to open the cupboard door, Marcia did smile. And Sue, watching in fascination, thought she looked like a cat which had just seen a bird—with only one leg.

The last two lessons of the afternoon were called Expressive Arts, and Sue and the others went to Drama, though they had to change subjects each term so that everybody took their fair share of Mrs Gipsum's Music. On their way along the covered space which led to the Drama hall, Rachel caught up with Matt and Danny. "Did you get a look at the register?" she asked. "I was dying to know all through Maths, but you know what Mr Watts is like."

"It was still blank," said Matt. "Her name was in, but nothing else."

"Oh, blow," said Rachel. Mr Potter is so inefficient. Even if he is lovely," she added in self-mockery.

"It might be the office," said Matt. "I mean, he can't put her address in until he knows it."

"Come *on*!" called Mrs Palgrave from the door of the Drama hall. "Don't be such slowcoaches!"

"She looks like something out of a fairy story," said Sue. "All that long fair hair. Who was that girl who leaned out of a tower to let someone climb up her hair?"

"Rapunzel," said Rachel. "It must have hurt. I wouldn't do that for anyone."

"You couldn't," said Danny, reaching up to ruffle Rachel's short, curly mop of dark hair. She turned round to swat at him as if he was an irritating bluebottle, and Mrs Palgrave beckoned energetically. "Hurry *up*," she shouted. "I've got lots to tell you!" She wore black trousers and a black sweat shirt with a 'Save the Whale' badge on it.

"Good!" said Rachel, quickening her pace. "If there's one thing, I like, it's news."

When they were all in the hall, Mrs Palgrave said, "Right! Everyone sit down."

There was a prolonged clatter as the tip-up seats in the tiered auditorium were banged down. Marcia came in last and stood inside the door, glaring at what she obviously considered to be a rabble.

"Hello!" said Mrs Palgrave, interested. "Who's this?"

"The Queen of Sheba," said Danny, grinning.

"Oh, don't be like that," said Mrs Palgrave. "Come along in, dear—don't be shy!" Everyone snorted with amusement at the thought of Marcia being shy, and she advanced into the hall, clutching her orange bag in both arms.

"She's jolly well going to *look* shy now Mrs Palgrave's suggested it," said Rachel to Sue.

"Has your bag got a broken handle?" enquired Mrs Palgrave sympathetically.

"'Sall right," said Marcia, waif-like.

"Oh. The way you're carrying it, I thought it had collapsed. What's your name, dear?"

"Marcia Mudd."

There were renewed giggles and Danny was heard to say, "Her name is Mud."

Marcia turned on him. "Think you're so clever, don't you?" she shouted. "If you want to know, people been saying that ever since I was five. Gets boring."

"And I think it's very unkind," said Mrs Palgrave. "I'm surprised at you, Danny. Sit down, Marcia dear. Now, everyone listen, because I want to tell you about the pantomime."

"Are we doing one for Christmas?" asked Rachel eagerly.

"Yes, we are."

"We went to a pantomime last year," said John Beasley suddenly. "Aladdin, it was. There was these two men papering a wall and—"

"Hang on," said Mrs Palgrave. "Save it up, John. Any ideas may be useful. The point about our pantomime is that we are going to make it up ourselves because that's the way all pantomimes are invented, and we want *everyone* to help. Not just children in the school, but older brothers and sisters, and mums and dads and friends—everyone."

"And teachers?" asked Rachel.

"Oh, definitely teachers," agreed Mrs Palgrave.

Rachel looked disappointed. "If *they're* going to be in it, there won't be any good parts for us," she protested.

"Of course there will," Mrs Palgrave assured her. "We'll need a girl with nice legs and a good voice to be the Principal Boy and—"

"A girl to be a boy?" interrupted Peter Box. "That's daft!"

"The Principal Boy is always a girl, stupid," said Marcia unexpectedly. "Same as the Dame is always a bloke."

"That's right," said Mrs Palgrave, smiling. "I'm glad someone knows a bit about the theatre. Do you like acting, Marcia?"

"Don't mind," said Marcia. Then she added, "My mother's an actress."

"*Is* she?" Mrs Palgrave was impressed. "What's her name?"

"It can't be Mudd," Danny muttered to Matt.

"Gloria York," said Marcia.

"Goodness," said Mrs Palgrave politely. "I can't say I've actually seen her in anything, but it seems to ring a bell."

"Has she been on telly?" asked John.

"She makes films," Marcia told him. "Abroad."

"Can't she speak English, then?" enquired Rachel nastily.

"Oh, ha, ha," snarled Marcia.

"Rachel! What a beastly thing to say!" Mrs Palgrave looked very shocked. "I don't want to hear anything else like that. Now, I thought our pantomime could be Cinderella. With any luck, you see, we'll get some fathers interested, and some of the men on the staff, so we'll have plenty of talent to pick from for the Ugly Sisters."

"You mean—" began Peter.

"Yes, they're played by men," Mrs Palgrave told him. "It's all part of the pantomime tradition, as Marcia said. That's what makes it such fun. Miss Duffy says she'll produce a comic ballet with men dressed up in frilly skirts and pink tights."

"Who's Miss Duffy?" whispered Danny.

"Teaches Girls' PE," Felicity told him. "Not Mrs Fawcett —the young one with short hair. Dark."

Danny nodded. "Oh, yes."

Everyone was laughing at the idea of the men wearing frilly skirts. "Be good if one of them was Mr Watts!" said Stephen Chuff.

"I don't think he would do it, somehow," said Mrs Palgrave regretfully. "The PE men are quite willing, but they're too good at it, if you know what I mean. It would be much funnier with men who've never done any Dance or Movement."

"What about Mr Potter?" suggested Rachel.

"Yes, he's nice and bumbly," agreed Mrs Palgrave. "And there might be some real talent among the dads. We're going to hold a meeting next week for any parents who are interested —there'll be a notice in Assembly. What about your dad, Marcia? Would he like to help us, do you think?"

Marcia glanced at the others from under her eyelashes, clearly indicating that she dared not answer for fear of ridicule from the rest of the class.

"Ooh," muttered Rachel. "Couldn't you murder her?"

Mrs Palgrave smiled at Marcia encouragingly. "You mustn't be afraid to speak up, dear," she said. "Do be sure to ask your dad to come along—and your mother, too, if she's not working. Apart from anything else, it's such a nice way to get to know people, isn't it? I expect you're new to the district, are you?"

Marcia managed to look forlorn. "Yeah," she said.

"She's just pretending," whispered Sue, half in outrage and half in reluctant admiration.

"Getting round Mrs Palgrave like that," Rachel muttered furiously. "It's maddening."

"Now," said Mrs Palgrave. "Before we can cast this pantomime, we'll have to assemble lots of ideas. The great thing about pantomime, you see, is that you can put what you like in it. If you've got a good singer, for instance, you can put him or her in as an entertainer at the Ball. You can include any kind of comedy sketch or dance routine or—or juggling, or someone who can play a penny whistle—anything!"

"Who's going to be Cinderella?" asked Rachel.

"I'll hold auditions for the major parts," said Mrs Palgrave. "There'll be a list on the English notice board, and anyone who wants to try can put their name down. Cinders herself needs to be a fairly thin girl, not too big. She's got to be able to look pathetic." She laughed at the instant expression of tragedy which came over Rachel's face and said, "All right, I get the message! You might do for Cinders, Rachel, but you'll have to take your chance with the rest."

"Sue, you ought to try for the Fairy Godmother," said Rachel. "You'd like turning mice into pumpkins."

"Oh, I couldn't!" said Sue. "Out there in front of all those people—I'd die of fright. And the mice were footmen, not pumpkins." John Beasley had started a rambling account of the wallpapering scene from Aladdin, and Sue saw Marcia glance up at Mrs Palgrave with a glint of amusement which caused the Drama teacher to smile in return. "I bet Marcia will get a good part," she said to Rachel. "You can see Mrs Palgrave thinks she's wonderful."

"Oh, no!" groaned Rachel. "I couldn't act with *her*!"

Mrs Palgrave clapped her hands loudly, tossing her long hair back from her shoulders. "All shush," she said. "Or you won't know what we're going to do." She picked up a sheaf of exercise paper from the edge of the stage behind her and said, "I want everyone to write down any idea they may have which might be useful for the pantomime. It can be about a person they know who can do something—in the school or out of it—or it can be an idea for something funny, or perhaps a mechanical idea. It could be a way to transform a pumpkin into a coach, or a design for a mouse-footman costume—"

Sue nudged Rachel and said, "See?"

"—or a dance for a pantomime horse, or—"

"Oh, I'd love to be a horse!" cried Felicity.

"Back legs or front legs?" asked Stephen.

"Front legs," said Felicity at once. "If I was the back legs I couldn't see where I was going."

"Or anything like John's wallpapering, that you've seen someone else do and think we might adapt. Then there are all the technical jobs," Mrs Palgrave went on. "We'll need people to paint the scenery and make the costumes and do the lights and prompt and—"

"What's prompt?" asked Danny. "Make sure they all get there on time?"

"No, make sure they don't forget their words," Mrs Palgrave told him. "The prompter sits just offstage with the script, so if anyone dries—runs out of words, that is—the prompter tells them their next line."

"I wouldn't mind that," said Sue.

"I'd hate it," said Rachel. "If I can't be in it, with a decent part, then I don't want anything to do with it at all."

Almost involuntarily, she glanced over at Marcia, whose dark-ringed eyes met hers with an identical expression of determination. And Sue, looking from one girl to the other, realised that, when it came to acting, the two of them shared exactly the same ambition.

CHAPTER 3

What is Entertainment?

When the bus from Tavenham arrived at Mill Green the next morning, Rachel stared round as they got out and said, "No sign of the Rolls yet."

"You'd think they'd have a chauffeur," said Sue. "In a proper uniform, with gold buttons."

"The man who was driving it yesterday didn't look like a chauffeur," said Matt. "Do you think he was Marcia's dad?"

"He must have been," said Sue. "I mean, he *looked* like her dad."

"I wouldn't be too sure," said Rachel darkly.

"But he couldn't be a boyfriend," Sue protested. "He's about forty!"

"So?" enquired Rachel.

Matt grinned. "So you've got a great imagination, Rachel!"

"Her mother wouldn't let her go out with anyone that age," said Sue. "Mine wouldn't, anyway."

"Your mum's not Gloria York, is she?" said Rachel. "I expect actresses have different ideas from people like your mum. If she *is* an actress, that is."

They were walking across the bus park to the first year entrance door, which was at the far side of a paved area edged with red-berried shrubs. Parallel to the way they were walking was a single-storey wing of the building containing two classrooms, the first of which was Mr Potter's room. Sue glanced casually across at the big windows—and clutched Rachel's arm. "Look!" she said. Through the glass they could see the unmistakeable red head of Marcia Mudd.

"The Rolls must have come and gone, then," said Matt.

"'S'pose so." Rachel sounded rather disappointed. "What's she doing?"

Marcia was sitting on a desk with her feet propped on

another one. She seemed to be attending to something closely.

"I think she's painting her fingernails," said Felicity.

"Mr Watts will do his nut!" said Danny.

Rachel marched purposefully through the swing doors and along the corridor. She pushed open the door of Mr Potter's room and said, "'Morning!"

"Oh," said Marcia, wiggling her fingers in the air to dry her nails. "There you are. I wondered if anyone was coming."

"You're early," said Matt.

"Dad on early turn at the factory, was he?" enquired Rachel kindly.

For a moment, Marcia's fingers were still. Then she waved her hand airily again and said, "My dad has a very important meeting this morning. With the other directors of the company."

"What's he do, then?" asked Danny.

"He's in the entertainments business," said Marcia. Everyone looked puzzled. She screwed the top back on her bottle of pink nail varnish and spread her fingers admiringly. "That should keep 'em happy," she remarked.

"It won't," said Matt with contempt. "You're not allowed to wear *any* kind of nail varnish."

"Well, tough," said Marcia. "I got to, that's all, or my nails split." She was still wearing her earrings.

"Actually," observed Rachel, "it's the varnish that makes them split. My mother had that trouble and she found out that there's something in the varnish that lots of people are allergic to. And most people never realise it's the varnish, so they go on using it to cover up the splits. Great for the people who make nail varnish but lousy for your nails."

Marcia looked at her in a bored way. They she said, "Load of cobblers, that is. I suppose your mum's one of these health freaks, is she?"

"Sort of," agreed Sue rashly.

"She's *not*!" said Rachel furiously. "She's got the sense not to waste money on rubbish that doesn't agree with her, that's all!"

"What's Entertainments, anyway?" asked Danny. "I mean, what does your dad actually *do*?"

"Telly's entertainment, innit," said John. "And films and that."

"Yes, but I want to know—" Danny began. But at that moment Mr Potter came in with the register under his arm. "'Morning!" he said cheerfully. "Sit down quickly—it's Assembly this morning and we always seem to be the last lot into the common room. Sit *down*, Danny."

As she went to her place, Rachel gave Sue a resentful stare and Sue wished she had kept her mouth shut. Still, she told herself, it was quite true. Rachel's mother *was* a bit of a health freak.

Dawdling along the corridor on his way to the office, Matt opened the register carefully and looked along the list of names. There was still no address beside Marcia's name. He closed the register again, pondering deeply. He knew what Rachel would say. "Why didn't you tell them in the office to fill it in? You could have said Mr Potter was waiting for it or something." Matt tried to imagine himself asking for Marcia's address on Mr Potter's behalf, and knew that he couldn't do it. He would turn red and stammer. And what if they told Mr Potter he had asked? The very thought of it made Matt blush to the roots of his fair hair. He reached the office and put the register carefully on top of the pile of others. The secretary, typing busily, did not even notice he was there.

Fortunately, Rachel was too excited about the pantomime to ask about Marcia's address. During Assembly Mr Hazzard repeated all that Mrs Palgrave had said about the staff and parents being involved as well as the children. "As I have told you before," he said, "I feel that a school should be much more than just a place where children come between the hours of nine and four. It should be open to everyone, a centre where people can come together to do all sorts of things—sport, drama, music. Anything at all. There will be a meeting next Friday evening for anyone interested. Notices will be given out by form tutors tomorrow."

"Yes, but when are they having the auditions?" Rachel muttered impatiently.

Mr Hazzard went on to say that anyone wanting to try for a part in the pantomime should put his or her name on the list on the English notice board, following which auditions would be arranged. "And now," he concluded, "we will sing hymn number one-six-two, 'Brightest and Best of the Sons of the Morning'."

"Come on," said Rachel to Matt as they filed out of Assembly. "Let's go and put our names down for the pantomime."

"Not me," said Matt. "I hate acting. And you'd better wait until break, or you'll be late for History. And you know what Mrs Abbott's like."

"I don't care," said Rachel obstinately. "I want to get my name on the list. Suppose it all gets filled up by break time and Mrs Palgrave takes it down because she's got enough names?"

"She wouldn't do that," put in Sue. "I expect it'll be up for the rest of the week."

"All the same," Rachel insisted, "I'd rather make sure. Could you take my books to History? Then I won't have to go back to Mr Potter's room to collect them."

"OK," said Sue.

There were quite a lot of fifth and sixth formers round the notice board, debating in a lofty way whether they should join in Mrs Palgrave's end-of-term romp or not.

"'Scuse me," said Rachel, trying to wriggle through them to the board.

"Who is this pushy infant?" asked Roger Smart, who was six feet two inches tall and towered above Rachel.

"I just wanted to put my name down," said Rachel.

"We're *all* putting our names down," said Roger. "Probably."

"So just wait," added Judith Ellistone.

With mounting impatience, Rachel waited. At last the seniors decided that a pantomime was too frivolous a production to merit their attention, and drifted away. "There you are, little Sarah Bernhardt," said Judith over her plump shoulder. "It's all yours."

Rachel wrote her name boldly on the list and turned to go. Then for some reason she felt impelled to glance back at the sheet of paper. There, at the head of the list in large green felt-tip letters was the name—Marcia Mudd. Rachel stared at it, dumbfounded. So *that's* why the beastly girl had arrived so early! Angrily, Rachel walked back along the corridor. The school had that ominous quietness which meant that lessons had not only begun, but had settled into their stride.

". . . but many people were serfs," Mrs Abbott was saying as Rachel opened the door. Sue covertly pointed a finger at the empty desk beside her, indicating to Rachel that her books were waiting for her there.

Mrs Abbott turned her full attention to the latecomer. "*Well*?" she demanded.

"Sorry I'm late, miss," said Rachel.

"Eight and a half minutes late. Just *what* have you been doing?"

A variety of plausible excuses ran through Rachel's head but she decided that the truth sounded virtuous enough to allay Mrs Abbott's wrath. "I had to put my name on Mrs Palgrave's list," she explained. "And there were a lot of older people there in front of me so —"

"What do you mean, 'had to'?" enquired Mrs Abbott coldly. "The truth is, you found some attractive alternative to work and made the most of it."

Rachel tried again. "No, honestly," she said. "I couldn't get near the board and—"

"I never heard such rubbish," said Mrs Abbott. "Being a born show-off, you can't wait to get yourself into the pantomime, can you? If your marks were half as high as your opinion of yourself it would be all right, but as it is, Mr Hazzard will probably feel that your time would be better spent in improving your work."

Rachel gazed at her, stricken. Did Mrs Abbott mean that she wouldn't be *allowed* to take part in the pantomime?

"Sit down!" snapped Mrs Abbott, pointing at an empty desk at the front of the class.

"Er—my books are—" Rachel indicated Sue and the desk beside her

"I see." Mrs Abbott pursed her lips. "Not only are you late, but you had *planned* to be late, asking your friend to bring your books for you." She surveyed the rows of desks and settled on Marcia, who sat directly in front of the empty desk beside Sue. "New girl—what's your name?"

"Marcia, miss," said Marcia politely.

"Bring those books from the desk behind you. Yes, that's right—bring them up here."

Marcia approached, carrying the books. She walked with small, modest steps, looking diffident and utterly virtuous in spite of the gypsy earrings and the outrageously bright red hair.

"You are not allowed to wear earrings in this school," said Mrs Abbott. "Didn't you know that?"

"No, miss!" said Maria innocently.

"Then bear it in mind in future. Put the books down there."

"Yes, miss," said Marcia. As she turned to go back to her place she narrowed her eyes and poked out her tongue at Rachel. Debbie Smart, sitting in the front row, gave an involuntary squeak and quickly turned it into a cough. Several of the boys laughed. Rachel sat down beside Debbie in the allocated desk, red-faced, and Mrs Abbot, who had not observed Marcia's insult, picked up a stick of chalk and returned to her list of headings on the blackboard. "Now," she said, "if Rachel Greenberg has quite finished her interruption, we will go on with the barons and serfs. By the way, Rachel, I will expect an essay on the life of a serf, on my desk, first thing tomorrow morning."

"Yes, miss," said Rachel stoically.

"Honestly," fumed Rachel at break time, "it's a bit much."

"She's so snooty," agreed Danny.

"You should have seen the face she made at Rachel!" said Stephen, grinning.

"Beastly," agreed Sue. "And after looking so innocent when Mrs Abbott was looking, too. That's what gets me—she's such a good actress."

"That's not being a good actress," objected Rachel. "That's just plain nasty."

Some of the boys were playing handball against the end wall of the classroom block, which was the only wall without windows in it.

"It's all very well playing handball," said Rachel. "*I* think we ought to do something about Marcia."

"So do I," said Stephen. "She makes me sick."

"Me, too," agreed Matt.

"She's *beastly* to Rachel,' said Sue.

"She's not the only one," said Rachel darkly.

"Why?" asked Sue, blushing.

"I don't know if you're my friend or hers," complained Rachel. "You've gone all funny."

"Oh, I haven't, Rachel!" Sue protested.

As the bell went, Danny dashed across in pursuit of a missed ball. "Come on!" he shouted back to the others. "It's PE next! Better go and get changed!"

Rachel's mood of despondency did not lift. "I don't know," she said as they started back to the building. "It's easy to *say* you're someone's friend. Proving it is something different."

Felicity and Debbie had caught up with them. "You do ask a lot, Rachel," observed Felicity. "Poor old Sue—how *can* she prove it? And why should she, anyway?"

Sue's round face was puckered with determination. "I *will* prove it," she said. "Just you wait and see."

Miss Duffy, who had been on duty, bounced past them wearing a maroon tracksuit with white stripes round the shoulders. "Come on, you lot!" she shouted cheerfully. "Wake up!"

"She makes me wish I *was* asleep," said Rachel. "I might just as well be. She's got enough energy for both of us."

"See you in a minute," said Sue. She ran ahead of them into the building.

"What's the matter with her?" asked Debbie, surprised. "She's not usually keen to get changed—specially when it's hockey."

"I don't know," said Rachel gloomily. "There's something the matter with everybody since Little Miss You-know-who arrived. Where is she, anyway?" She looked round at the emptying field, but there was no sign of Marcia.

"I expect she's smoking in the loo," said Felicity.

"I hope it kills her," muttered Rachel. Everyone laughed.

"Oh, come on," said Felicity, quickening her pace. "We'd better hurry or Miss Duffy will be jumping up and down."

"She *always* jumps up and down," said Rachel, who was determined not to cheer up.

"Come on!" said Miss Duffy, bursting into the changing room, "you should all be ready by now." She herself had taken off her tracksuit and now appeared in a short navy skirt, striped socks and hockey boots. She was small and very slim, and seemed to move twice as fast as anyone else. Most people liked her, and the girls who were ready crowded to the door. Sue was still busy doing up the laces of her training shoes, and Marcia, sitting slumped on a bench with her arms folded, had made no attempt to change at all.

"You're new, aren't you?" said Miss Duffy, approaching her.

"Yeah," said Marcia.

Miss Duffy looked at her. "M'm," she said, "I did hear that you were inclined to be a bit rude. Marcia Mudd, isn't it?"

"'Sright," said Marcia, not moving.

"Well, please unfold your arms, Marcia, and get your PE kit on. Where *is* your kit?"

"Someone pinched it," said Marcia.

"Oh, what rubbish! Did you forget to bring it?"

"No, I brought it all right," said Marcia, "but me trainers has gone. Me bag's still here, look, and me tracksuit and all that."

"Then put your tracksuit on and get outside," said Miss Duffy crisply.

"Not coming out in all that mud in me good shoes," said Marcia, indicating her black, high-heeled shoes with slender ankle straps. Miss Duffy sighed. "Those are *not* good shoes," she said patiently. "Shoes like that are very bad for your feet. If you turn your ankle you could easily pull a ligament and have endless trouble with it."

"That's my problem," retorted Marcia.

"Oh, no, it's not," Miss Duffy persisted. "It's the school's problem, because it's our job, among other things, to keep you fit so you can come here every day and do your lessons. So don't give me that. Now, where *are* your trainers?"

"I told you," snapped Marcia. "They bin took. I went to the loo and when I come back they was gone. And that's the truth, and if you don't like it, stuff it."

For a moment, Rachel thought Miss Duffy was going to hit Marcia, and glanced round to see if Sue was appreciating this dramatic moment. But Sue, unnoticed by anyone else, had gone out. She certainly was keen on PE this morning, Rachel thought.

Miss Duffy's lips tightened but she stepped back from Marcia and merely said, pointing at the door, "Out."

"Out where?" asked Marcia, getting up languidly.

"Out to the paved area," said Miss Duffy. "OK, you can keep your silly heels out of the mud, but exercise you jolly well will. Round and round the flowerbeds. And I'm going to watch you."

Marcia went out, muttering.

"Right," said Miss Duffy. "All you sluggards, out you go as well." She paused and added, "Nobody *did* pinch her shoes, did they?"

"No, we didn't," said Rachel. "Honestly."

"I'm glad," said Miss Duffy with a hint of menace.

During the hockey game Marcia walked about reluctantly on the paved area, shoulders hunched and arms folded across her chest. From time to time she would stop and lean against a wall, glaring at the ground, but each time this happened Miss Duffy noticed within a few minutes. And when Marcia saw the little PE mistress come running across the grass towards her she would lever herself away from the wall and resume her moody pacing.

At last Miss Duffy blew her whistle for the end of the lesson and everyone ran back to the changing room.

"Before I turn the showers on," shouted Miss Duffy above the general chatter, "I want to see everyone's PE shoes. They should all have your names in."

There was a general groan.

"These aren't marked," Miss Duffy said to Sue as she inspected her shoes. "They are yours, are they?"

"Yes," said Sue, blushing crimson.

"What size are they?"

"Four," said Sue.

"What size do you take, Marcia?" called Miss Duffy.

"Five," said Marcia. "And mine was new."

"Right," said Miss Duffy. "Make sure these are marked, Sue. It saves an awful lot of bother if you lose them."

Two other pairs of shoes were not marked, but Marcia said neither of them were hers. "Mine was brand new," she said again. "Really good ones, white with red stripes. My dad don't buy no rubbish."

"Then you'd better have a thorough hunt for them," said Miss Duffy. "And when you find them, take better care of them."

She hopped up on a bench beside the shower pipes, put the key in the master tap by the ceiling and turned it. Water burst forth from the rows of showers in the cubicles and in a few minutes the tiled room was full of steam.

"You've got six minutes," shouted Miss Duffy as she went out. "So you'd better hurry up!"

Rachel was feeling distinctly better. She rammed her damp towel into her sports bag and said to Sue, "Come on! Let's go and see what the dreaded Marcia's up to." Marcia, ignoring the showers, had gone straight out as soon as Miss Duffy had left the changing room.

"I don't think I want to," said Sue.

"Why not?" asked Rachel. "She'll be in the dining area—we can tease her a bit while we have our dinner. Oh, come on, Sue! Honestly, she's so stuck-up, she makes me boil."

"I know," said Sue unhappily. "But it's all right now, after the shoes business, isn't it? She didn't like that a bit."

Rachel looked at her friend sharply, and Sue's round, honest face crimsoned again as she tried to look unconcerned.

"*Sue!*" said Rachel accusingly. "It was *you*, wasn't it?

That's why you rushed in from the field at break, to swipe her shoes!"

Sue nodded. She suddenly looked as if she was going to cry.

"Well, you were trying to get Sue to prove she was your friend, Rachel," Debbie pointed out.

"Oh, *Sue*!" Rachel looked contrite. "I didn't mean it seriously. Silly old thing!"

"Well, I think it's great," said Felicity. "I wish I'd thought of it."

Sue sniffed. "Do you really?" she asked.

"'Course she does," said Debbie. "So do I. Time someone took Marcia down a peg or two."

"I can't believe it!" said Rachel, grinning. "I always thought you were such a mouse, Sue! Where did you put them?"

"What?" asked Sue, confused.

"The shoes, twit!"

"Oh. I gave them to Danny."

"Danny! What was *he* doing in here?"

"He wasn't. I came in and her stuff was lying all over the place and she was in the loo. I hadn't planned what I was going to do. I just wanted to—do something to her. Anything." They all nodded understandingly. "And there were these posh trainers," Sue went on, "lying on the bench near my things. So I thought I'd hide them somewhere so she'd have to look for them—but there's nowhere you *can* hide anything in here, is there? Then I heard Danny and Peter outside, arguing about that handball game they were playing. So I gave the shoes to Danny and told him to put them in his bag."

"What did he say?" asked Debbie.

"Nothing," said Sue. "I think he got the idea, 'cos he just went straight off into the boys' changing room."

"Brilliant," said Rachel. "What do we do next?"

"What do you mean?" asked Sue.

"Well, we can't just give them back to her," said Rachel. "But none of us want to be stuck with them. I mean, we're not *stealing* them. We ought to put them in some silly place."

"In Mr Potter's desk?" suggested Felicity.

"No—too obvious we put them there," said Rachel. "It's got to be somewhere *she* might have put them, then if there's a row about it, she gets in the row and we don't."

"Um." They all thought.

"In the loo?" suggested Debbie.

"Could do, I suppose." Rachel was not enthusiastic. "Much better if it caused some bother when they were found. Now, who doesn't like her?"

"You don't," said Sue.

"No, among the teachers, I mean. Mrs Palgrave's no good, she thinks she's marvellous."

"Mr Watts doesn't," said Felicity.

"Mr Watts," said Rachel thoughtfully. "Wouldn't it be lovely to upset Mr Watts *and* Marcia!"

Somebody tapped at the changing room door. Sue, who was nearest, opened it and looked out.

"*There* you are!" said Danny. "Don't you girls take ages to change? What do you want to do with these?" He indicated his bulging sports bag. "I don't want to cart someone else's shoes about all day."

"We're just deciding," said Sue.

"Let's go and have some dinner," said Rachel. "I can't think when I'm hungry. Where are Matt and the others?"

"Gone across to the canteen," said Danny. "I've been waiting here forages."

"Never mind," said Rachel. "I'm going to have a really good idea, I know I am. And you can be part of it."

"I was afraid of that," said Danny. And they all set off towards the canteen.

CHAPTER 4

Sue's Proof

Marcia sat by herself at lunch, between a group of sixth formers who ignored her and a gang of fourth year boys who did not.

"'Ullo, darling," one of them said. "What you doing tonight?"

Marcia took no notice.

"Where d'you live?" asked another one. "I'll come round yours and pick you up."

"He's marvellous," a third boy told Marcia. "All the girls say so, don't they, Ron?"

"And they're right," Ron boasted.

"Why don't you just leave me alone?" said Marcia sulkily. "I don't want anything to do with you, so shut up."

"Ooh!" said the boys, pained. "Don't want nothing to do with us! Snooty piece!"

"Listen, darlin'," said the boy called Ron, leaning across the table. "You *do* want something to do with us. Nobody gets born with their hair that colour, so why change it? I tell you why. 'Cos it's more attractive, that's why. Same as you paint your nails and wear trousers that tight you can see where your knickers end. You do it to make the boys look. So it's no good going all hard-to-get when they do. See?"

"Oh, shut up," said Marcia.

Sue, observing from a distance, nudged Rachel and said, "She looks quite upset."

"She couldn't be upset if she tried," said Rachel. But, looking up, she saw Marcia jump to her feet, red-faced, and push her way past the boys amid laughter and cat-calls.

"I think those fourth years were more than she bargained for," said Matt, as Marcia almost ran out of the dining area.

"Good for them," said Stephen. "If a few more people tease her, she might stop pretending to be so superior."

"Right," agreed Danny. "Now, what about these training shoes? I told you, I'm not—"

"Hang on," interrupted Rachel. She finished the last of her shepherd's pie and added, "M'm. That's better."

"But what—" Danny began again.

"Let's tie them to the bumper of the Rolls Royce," said Felicity. "Then it'll look as if she and her dad have just got married."

"And you think Marcia's dad is just going to sit there and let you do it?" enquired Rachel. She thought and admitted, "It's a nice idea, though." Then she snapped her fingers. "I know! Not the Rolls—Mr Watts's Mini! With a notice saying, 'Marcia Mudd loves Mr Watts'."

"Oh, we can't," said Sue.

"Of course we can," scoffed Rachel. "Look, he parks his car round the corner in that little bit outside the Head's office. It's reserved for Mr Hazzard and the Senior Mistress and Mr Watts."

"Senior Master," Stephen explained.

"I know," said Sue. "And the secretaries use it, too. But—"

"There's no windows look out that way except Mr Hazzard's," Rachel went on, "and he's always in the staff room at lunch time because he likes to be friendly with everyone. I think it's lovely, really. Most headmasters aren't like that a bit."

"But what are we going to *do*?" persisted Danny.

"Go out now, as soon as you've finished schlooping up all that custard, and tie the trainers on his bumper. You can do the tying and I'll do the notice and someone can keep a lookout."

"I will," said Stephen.

"That's it, then," said Rachel. "All settled. I think I'll have a banana."

She pushed her chair back and wriggled her way between the rows of diners until she reached the open space by the hatch, where there was no longer any queue.

Sue sighed. "I wish Rachel wouldn't keep doing such mad things."

"No, you don't," said Debbie. "You love it. Otherwise you wouldn't have made all that effort to prove you were her friend."

Sue gazed at her dubiously. Then she peeled the lid off her pot of strawberry yoghurt and licked it carefully. Life was very confusing sometimes, she thought.

The plan was surprisingly easy to carry out. As Rachel had said, there was nobody about in that part of the school and so there was plenty of time to affix the notice and the red-and-white striped shoes. Mr Watts's Mini wore a slightly raffish air when they left it, and Sue gigled. "Poor little car," she said. "I bet it's never done anything like that before in its life."

"With any luck," said Stephen, "he'll come out of the door by the Head's office, straight to the front of the car, get in and drive off."

"And he'll never notice!" said Matt. "Great!"

"Come on," said Danny, ever energetic in spite of his small size. "We've got time for another game of handball before the bell goes."

When he collected the register from the office to take up to Mr Potter's room that afternoon, Matt opened it as usual to see if the blank space beside Marcia Mudd's name had been filled in—and it had. He stopped in his tracks, causing Mr Fox to collide with him from behind.

"For Heaven's sake, boy," grumbled Mr Fox. "You want brake lights or something, if you're going to do that."

"Sorry, sir," said Matt. He moved aside, where nobody else was likely to fall over him, and opened the register again. The neatly-written letters jumped before his eyes. "19, Prospect Row, Bosworth Estate, Flaxton." Matt read it twice, amazed. There was no way that anyone could describe a house in Prospect Row as being "a place in the country". So what was going on? He returned to Mr Potter's room thoughtfully.

Rachel saw at once that Matt's face looked unusually pink and excited under his thatch of fair, floppy hair. "What's up?" she asked across the classroom "Is it in?" Matt nodded and went to his place.

"Quiet!" shouted Mr Potter.

"But, Matt," Rachel went on loudly. "What does it *say*? I want to know!"

"Rachel!" protested Mr Potter. "Will you please stop talking? It's bad enough at the best of times, without you putting your oar in!"

"Sorry," said Rachel impatiently. She sat with her hands gripped tightly together as Mr Potter read through the list of names, looking as if she was about to blow up.

"Now," said Mr Potter as he entered the total and closed the register. "I've got these forms for your parents to fill in saying whether they want to come to the meeting about the pantomime. Anybody got a mum who's an ex-filmstar?"

"Marcia has," said Debbie.

"Really?" Mr Potter looked interested. "Is that right, Marcia."

"Yeah," said Marcia. "Not 'ex', though. She's filming in America."

"Well, well, well!" said Mr Potter, obviously thrilled. He took off his glasses and wiped them, then put them on again.

"What sort of films does she make?"

"Well . . . they're a bit special," said Marcia. "They don't always get shown in England."

"Educational, perhaps?" suggested Mr Potter.

"Something like that," said Marcia.

Mr Potter smiled. "You'll find there's lots of enthusiasm for drama in this school," he said. "I expect you'll make heaps of friends once you find a common interest."

"She'll be lucky," muttered Rachel.

And Marcia, smiling non-committally down at her pink nails said under her breath, "Don't know as I want to."

Matt told Rachel and the others about Marcia's address as they were walking along the corridor to Miss Harker's RE lesson.

"Prospect Row!" said Rachel. "Matt, are you sure?"

"Absolutely," said Matt. "I read it twice. Number nineteen Prospect Row, Bosworth Estate, Flaxton."

"But the Bosworth Estate is the grimmest council estate in the whole of Flaxton," said Rachel. "Some of them are lovely, but—"

"And Prospect Row is the worst street in it," agreed Stephen. "They pinch the wheels off your car if you leave it there more than an hour. My dad knows someone it happened to."

"Well, I live in a council house," said Debbie, "and so does Felicity, and our estate's fine, but we wouldn't go down Prospect Row after dark."

"My dad says the council put people there sometimes if they've made a mess of a better place," said Felicity, "or if it's a family who desperately need a house and they can't find anything better straight away. People like that usually get moved somewhere else quite soon, though."

Rachel was frowning in perplexity. "I don't understand it," she said. "There's something really funny going on."

They arrived at the door of Miss Harker's room. Bill North pushed open the door and looked in. The room was empty and Sue said, "We'd better wait outside."

"It's only Miss Harker," said Peter Box. "She won't mind."

They all went in and sat down, talking noisily.

"Where's Marcia?" asked Rachel, looking round. "I want to talk to her."

"Probably in the science block," said Peter smugly. "She asked me where RE was, in her snooty way. 'I don't suppose you know where this Miss 'Arker's room is, do you?'—and I said I thought it was number thirty-six."

"That's the Senior Biology lab!" said Stephen. "She'll get an awful telling-off from Mr Thomas if she walks in there!"

"That's what I thought," said Peter with satisfaction.

"What if it's all lies?" said Rachel, frowning. "All this bit about her mother being an actress in Hollywood and her father running a big business—"

"In Entertainments," said Danny. "She never did say what that meant."

"And the gold taps and the house in the country and the Rolls Royce. What if it's all made up?"

"But we've seen the Rolls Royce," Matt pointed out

"Yes," admitted Rachel. "Only once, though."

"P'raps they won the pools," said John Beasley.

Rachel stared at him thoughtfully. "Yes," she said slowly. "That could explain why she doesn't seem like someone who grew up rich. It must be something like that. But whatever it is, I'm going to find out."

At that moment Marcia came through the door, clutching her orange bag in both arms as usual, her chin up as if to prove that she didn't care what anyone said to her, even if he *was* the senior Biology master.

"Thanks a bunch," she said to Peter. "Very funny."

"Did I get it wrong?" asked Peter innocently.

"You know you got it wrong," said Marcia, sitting down at an empty desk. Rachel slid across and sat beside her. "There's something I want to ask you," she said.

"Oh, yeah?" Marcia looked wary.

"Yeah," Rachel repeated, mocking. "Nineteen, Prospect Row, that's what I want to ask you. Hardly a big place in the country, is it?"

Marcia stared at her, eyes narrowed under their dark-shadowed lids. Her eyelashes were spiky with mascara.

"Well, come on," insisted Rachel. "Do you live there or don't you?"

"Of course I don't," said Marcia. "That's where our cook lives. I told Dad to give that address when we come here. Stop nosy parkers interfering in our business. He said it was a good idea."

"I bet he did," said Rachel. For once, she was too confused by this ready answer to think of anything else to say. "I still think it sounds funny, though," she muttered as she went back to sit beside Sue.

Miss Harker came in, looking flustered. "I'm so sorry," she said to nobody in particular. "I was looking in the stock cupboard for the 'Religion Today' books and I can't see them anywhere. I was sure they ought to be there . . ."

But everyone was much too busy discussing Marcia's address to pay any attention to Miss Harker.

At going-home time everyone tried to get on the bus as slowly as possible, craning their necks to see if anyone had noticed the addition to Mr Watt's car.

"Right," said the bus driver, starting his engine. "I'm not waiting any longer. If there's any more of you late they'll just have to walk, that's all. We're blocking the way out for the other buses."

"Danny's not here," said Matt. "And his mum can't fetch him because his dad has the car all day."

"That's his tough luck," said the driver.

"Here he is!" shouted Rachel. Danny climbed aboard, panting. "Thanks for waiting," he said to the driver.

"More than you deserve," grumbled the driver, inching the bus forward. By this time several other buses had managed to edge past, but somebody's mother in a Ford Cortina had got into a muddle about backing out of her parking space, and nobody could move until her car was out of the way.

"I don't know," said the driver as he brought the bus to a halt again. "Some people didn't ought to be let out on their own."

There was a sound of impatient hooting from behind them and one of the fourth year boys called Terry Leveritt looked out of the rear window to see who it was.

"Mr Watts," he reported. "Seems to think it's the start of the Grand Prix or something."

"Oh, great!" said Danny, nudging Matt. "I wonder if he's noticed the shoes yet?"

Mr Watts hooted again.

"He's the same in his car as he is in his classroom," said Terry from the back. "Thinks everyone will do as they're told if he shouts loud enough."

The woman in the Cortina managed to get away at last, leaving deep tyre marks in the earth of the rosebed beside the parking space. Ollie Withett, the assistant caretaker, who had just dug the bed over, offered her his garden fork and invited her—none too politely—to make good the damage, but she accelerated away at speed, showering him with gravel.

"One born every minute," said the bus driver wearily. He glanced in his mirror and added, "Here comes another. Better let him through, I suppose." He slid the window back, put out his arm and waved Mr Watts past.

"Hey!" exclaimed Terry, who was still looking out of the window. "What's that on the back of his car?"

"Shoes," said his friend, Simon Wilson. He leaned out and bawled, "Oy, sir! You just got married?"

"Where's the confetti?" shouted Terry happily.

Mr Watts did not hear what was said, but as he passed each bus a laughing, jeering audience leaned out to shout comments and by the time he reached the gate he had obviously realised that something was wrong. He stopped the car and, regardless of the buses queued up behind him, got out, frowning. He looked at the bonnet and the front wheels, then walked round to the rear of the car. Angrily, he bent down and snatched at the training shoes, trying to jerk them off his bumper; but Danny had tied a very complicated knot and the shoes were difficult to remove. Ollie Withett came ambling up, garden fork over his shoulder, to see what was causing the new delay. Behind him, the buses hooted in derision. Baulked by the Mini, it was now their turn to show their impatience.

"Have you got a knife?" shouted Mr Watts at the approaching Ollie.

"I might have," said Ollie cautiously. He was about eighteen, with shaggy dark hair, and Mr Watts had on several occasions called him a teenage layabout.

"Well, have you or haven't you?" said Mr Watts irritably. "I want to cut these damned laces."

"Brand new shoes, aren't they?" remarked Ollie, unhurried. He bent down and began to fumble with the knots. "Pity to spoil them," he explained. Then he said, "Oh, look. There's a note in this shoe." He straightened up, with the piece of paper in his hand.

"Read it out, Ollie!" shouted Terry from the Tavenham bus.

Ollie glanced up. Then he read out carefully and loudly,

"I'm nuts about Mr Watts. But then, I'm nuts anyway. Marcia Mudd."

There were delighted cat-calls and wolf whistles from the buses as Mr Watts snatched the note from Ollie and rammed it into his pocket. "Get those shoes off there," he ordered. "And quick."

Ollie, sensing that Mr Watts was very close to explosion point, removed the shoes without any further delay, and handed them to the Senior Master.

"Thank you," snapped Mr Watts. He marched round to the Tavenham bus and shouted, "Is Marcia Mudd on this bus?"

"No!" chorused Danny and the others, weak with laughter.

Rachel managed to compose herself enough to add, "She goes home in a Rolls Royce, sir."

"Oh, *does* she?" snarled Mr Watts. "Does she indeed. Then will you kindly tell Miss Mudd I would like to see her in my room first thing tomorrow morning."

"Yes, sir," said Rachel, grinning.

The driver leaned across and said, "Look, *do* you mind moving your car, sir? You've finished your working day—I haven't. I got to pick up a load of drum majorettes at half-past five for a do in London, and I got to get to Tavenham and back first."

"All *right*," said Mr Watts. He stumped away and got in his car, which bucked a couple of times before proceeding out of the gate.

"He's so cross, he can't drive properly," said Matt. "What a laugh!"

The bus at last pulled out of the gate and started down the road. Glancing back across the grass to see how many other buses were delayed behind them, Sue suddenly noticed something.

"Rachel," she said, "look!"

"What?" Rachel followed her pointing finger to where a solitary figure, red-haired and carrying a large orange bag, was making its way down the drive to the gate.

"Marcia Mudd!" said Sue.

"Marcia Mudd," agreed Rachel. She sat back in her seat

thoughtfully. "Well," she said. "So what's happened to the Rolls Royce?"

"Perhaps it's gone in for service," suggested Matt.

"Rolls Royces don't need servicing," said Stephen. "Or hardly ever, anyway."

"Terry!" called Rachel, kneeling up to shout over the back of her seat to the fourth year boys in the rear. "Can you see if that girl with the orange bag is waiting at the gate?" Terry looked back along the straight road. "No," he reported. "She's walking the other way—towards Flaxton."

"Thanks," said Rachel, sitting down again. "What d'you bet she's going to Prospect Row?" she said to the others.

"Could be," Matt agreed. There was a general babble of speculation. Sue gazed silently out of the window, where the fields already began to show the speckled green lines of next year's wheat. There was something about Marcia which made her feel deeply unhappy. But, because she valued her friendship with Rachel, she dared not say so.

CHAPTER 5

Over The Top

The first two lessons the next morning were Art, with Mr Pebblemarsh, who came from Liverpool and seemed to regard life as a bad joke. "Right," he said, scratching the side of his reddish beard as he surveyed the class with disfavour, "Get sat down, then, and let's get started."

"Sir," Matt began eagerly, "are we going to—"

"Flippin' 'eck, mate," said Mr Pebblemarsh without loss of temper. "Give us a chance. There's this pantomime rearing its ugly head, and the powers that be want instant horror for the Hallowe'en shindig, and in between times I'm supposed to teach you lot some Art!"

"What Hallowe'en shindig?" asked Danny.

Mr Pebblemarsh put his finger to his lips and stared round the class through his rather bulgy eyes until everyone was attentive, though giggling slightly. "Hallowe'en," he said, "happens at the end of this month. It's the night when witches are supposed to ride and all sorts of ghosties and ghoulies and general nasties are about, and everyone enjoys scaring themselves witless. Now, our Mr Hazzard, being nothing if not a good businessman, thought we could raise some cash for our pantomime if we laid on a bit of a do on Hallowe'en night. Those lovely ladies in the cookery department are going to get sticky to the elbows with apples and toffee and I don't know what, while us serfs down here got to do the visuals."

"The what?" asked Peter.

"Visuals," repeated Mr Pebblemarsh. "What you *see*. A thing like Hallowe'en is a lot more fun if it *looks* good. So anyone rash enough to come into this Art room for the next few weeks is going to join the great nasties production team. What we're going to do—now listen, this is the nitty-gritty bit—we're going to have the place absolutely *hanging* with ghostly figures and witchy whatnots with long pointed fingers and all that sort of thing. Hey—and you know that creepy little corridor that goes from the back of the Drama hall round to the PE changing rooms?" They all nodded. "Well, we're going to turn that into a Horror Run," said Mr Pebblemarsh with relish. "Charge 'em two pence a time to be terrified."

"Five pence," said Rachel.

"What's it going to be like, then?" asked Sue.

"A bit like a ghost train at a fair," said Mr Pebblemarsh. "Only better. I mean, worse."

"Cor, smashing," said John Beasley.

"My mum wouldn't let me go on the ghost train when we were at the seaside," said Debbie. "She said I'd get nightmares."

"And so I should hope," said Mr Pebblemarsh, nodding his shaggy head enthusiastically. "No sense in a ghost train if you don't."

"The one I went on was silly," said Stephen. "You could see it was just lights flashing on and off, and paintings of skeletons and things, and then you went through a sort of curtain with dangly bits that brushed over you."

"Ugh!" said Felicity, shuddering.

"There you are, you see," said Mr Pebblemarsh. "Toughies like Stephen would have to have someone shooting their kneecaps off before they thought it was exciting, and other people get the heebies over a spider."

"*Don't*," said Sue.

"Main thing is to make a start," said Mr Pebblemarsh. "On this desk here there are huge sheets of my posh paper that comes on a roll so you don't have to fiddle about sticking small bits together. One stick of charcoal each, all ready for you beside the paper—and DON'T," he added, "let me hear the word, 'pencil'. Pencils have small points, so they're good for small drawings. These are going to be *large* drawings, afterwards painted. Work in groups, not more than four of you on one sheet of paper or you fetch up like council workmen."

"One digging the hole and the others watching," said Stephen.

"You've got it," agreed Mr Pebblemarsh. "Any questions?"

"What do we draw, sir?" asked Michael Chalmers. Mr Pebblemarsh sighed. "Somebody tell him," he said. "Now, get going." Dusting his hands together, he walked across the room to where Marcia sat on the edge of a table, looking out of the window.

"Well," he said. "You're a splendid lady to have in our midst. That's a marvellous colour you've done your hair. What's your name, love?"

"Marcia Mudd." Marcia did not look at him.

"Who's going to have Marcia in their group?" asked Mr Pebblemarsh generally. Everyone was suddenly very busy and did not appear to hear him.

"I don't want to be in any of their stinking groups," said Marcia. "Can't I be on my own?"

"It's a whopping great bit of paper to cover on your own," said Mr Pebblemarch.

"I'll just do a small one, then," said Marcia.

"Small ghosts aren't much cop," Mr Pebblemarsh objected. "Nobody's scared of a *small* ghost. Be better to do a little thing, only big, if you see what I mean. What about a spider? Do a spider, really giant, all hairy. If you want to see what they're like, there's a book on my shelf with pictures of tropical ones. Kill a horse with one bite."

"Don't mind," said Marcia.

Mr Pebblemarsh tore a sheet of paper in half and gave it to her, with a stick of charcoal. "Give us a shout if you want any help," he said. Then he turned his attention to Rachel and Sue, who had teamed up with Felicity and Debbie and were arguing about whether to draw a ghost or a witch, and what sort.

"Look here, I think we've got a bit of a House of Commons going on here," he said. "All talk and no do. Now, I want to start attacking that corridor as well, and the first thing is to get some screens down there, put sideways to the wall so as to break up the straightness. People will have to feel their way past them, you see."

"Will it be dark, then?" asked Rachel.

"Oh, yes, pitch-black," said Mr Pebblemarsh. "And hung about with creepy things that touch you, and hideous paintings that light up suddenly, and ghastly masks and tape-recorded noises—"

"I wouldn't mind shrieking," said Rachel. "And groaning and wailing. I could hide behind a picture of a ghost."

"Great!" said Mr Pebblemarsh. "But the first thing is to get the screens down there as a basis to work on. Can you lot give a hand, or shall I ask some boys?"

"Of course we'll help," said Rachel. "Coming, Sue?"

"I'd rather do this, really," said Sue apologetically.

"I'll move screens," Debbie decided.

"Me and Peter'll give a hand," Stephen offered from the next table.

"Right," said Mr Pebblemarsh. "I'll come and open the cupboard where the screens are kept and show you where to put them."

When Rachel and the others had gone out, Sue glanced across at Marcia, who looked up at that moment from her drawing of a spider and met Sue's eye. She let her gaze drift slowly down Sue's plump form, then up again. Then she returned to her spider.

Sue, blushing with embarrassment and a strange kind of hurt, wondered why she had worried about Marcia. Felicity glanced up at her across the table and said, "You're wasting your time with her, you know."

"Yes," said Sue miserably, "I think I am."

At break, Marcia was sitting on a bench outside, reading a lurid-looking magazine. Matt, walking past her, eating crisps, offered her the bag and said, "Want one?"

"No, thanks," said Marcia, still reading.

Matt sat down beside Marcia, who took no notice. After a few more crisps he said, "Look, what's going on? I mean, you do ask for trouble, don't you?"

"Oh, yeah?" said Marcia, turning a page.

"Everyone needs friends," Matt persisted. "I only moved

here from London last year, so I know. And our lot are OK really, to anyone who's reasonable. But you don't give anyone a chance."

"Who says I want to?" said Marcia indifferently.

"I do," said Matt firmly. "If you ask me, you're the same as all the rest of us. It's a load of rubbish, all this business about the house in the country and the gold taps. I don't think you've got anything to be stuck up about, so you might just as well—"

Marcia jumped to her feet. "Shut up!" she yelled. "Just shut up and leave me alone! I don't want any friends, and if I did, I wouldn't pick people who pinch your flaming shoes. So just mind your own—beastly—business!" With this last word she hurled the magazine at Matt, who was busy fishing the last crisp out of the bag. Marcia ran off towards the school, tripping and stumbling on her high heels as if, Matt thought incredulously, she was blinded by tears. He stared after her, then pitched his empty crisps bag in the bin.

Danny and Rachel came up excitedly.

"Did you see Marcia?" asked Danny. "She just rushed past us and it looked as if she was crying!"

"I know," said Matt.

"*Do* you?" asked Rachel. "But why? What did you say to her?"

"Nothing much," said Matt. "I just said people needed friends, so why didn't she come off it and stop being so snooty, and she just blew her top. Chucked this at me." He retrieved the magazine from the ground. "Stupid twit."

"She does get upset sometimes, then," said Rachel thoughtfully.

"She must have got an awful telling-off from Mr Watts if she went to see him about the shoes this morning," said Danny. "You know what he's like."

Rachel was still thinking. "There's more to it than that," she said. "I think that's why she makes me so cross. She puts on such an act of being posh, and I'm sure it's not true—but she won't let anyone find out what she's really like. I *will* find out, though—just you wait!"

Geography was a dull lesson about grasslands. Shading in green patches on an outline map of the world, Rachel told Sue in whispers about the incident with Marcia.

"I don't want to talk to her," Sue admitted. "I smiled at her in Art and she just looked at me as if I was something nasty. I felt really upset about it."

Danny sidled across and said, "Are you planning a treat for Marcia?"

"Look out," whispered Rachel, noticing that long thin Mr Ambrose was bearing down on them.

"Danny Williams, what are you doing out of your place?" asked Mr Ambrose severely.

"Want to borrow a rubber, sir," said Danny.

"Why haven't you got a rubber of your own?" grumbled Mr Ambrose. "It's not too much to ask that you people turn up equipped with the tools of your trade, but you can't even provide yourself with anything as basic as a rubber."

"I have got one, sir," said Danny, whose rubber was in his pencilcase. "It's just that I seem to have lost it."

"You're so careless," moaned Mr Ambrose, who always went on at length about this sort of thing. "Where did you last have it?"

"Don't know, sir," said Danny cheerfully.

"And you're so *scruffy*," Mr Ambrose complained. "Shoelaces undone, no tie, buttons missing off your jacket—*and* no rubber."

"I expect it will turn up," said Danny with confidence.

"When I was a boy," intoned Mr Ambrose, "we had to take care of things." Everyone grinned, having heard this so often before.

The door opened and a girl came in with a piece of paper.

"Yes?" said Mr Ambrose.

"Message from Mrs Palgrave, sir. She says there'll be a meeting in the Drama hall at quarter to one for anyone who's put their name down for the pantomime. There will be dinner-queue priority for people who want to come."

"You all heard that, did you?" Mr Ambrose asked the class. "Quarter to one."

"Will you sign it, sir?" said the girl, holding out the piece of paper. Mr Ambrose fiddled short-sightedly through the row of pens in his jacket pocket until he found the one he wanted, then added his name to the others at the bottom of the notice, certifying that it had duly been read out in his lesson. Clipping his pen back in his pocket as the girl went out, he said, "Reverting to the question of rubbers and other such equipment, it is important, you know, that you all have the appropriate . . ."

Everyone yawned and several people smothered groans.

Danny took his rubber out of his pencilcase, held it up and said happily, "Found it, sir!"

Mr Ambrose looked at him with hatred.

Rachel, dragging the reluctant Sue with her, was at the hatch as soon as the serving ladies slid it up. "Sausage and chips and beans, please," she said. "And one of those cakey things with spots on."

"Hundreds and thousands," said the lady.

"Can't be that many," said Rachel inanely. "And a cheese salad for Sue."

"I'm sick of cheese salad," said Sue. "I'm going to have egg and chips."

"That's right, dear," said the lady. "Don't you be bullied."

Rachel grinned and carried her tray to the cash desk.

"No sign of Marcia," said Sue when they had nearly finished their lunch. "Perhaps she's too upset to come to the pantomime meeting."

"Hope she jolly well is upset," said Rachel.

Matt and Danny and Stephen came to join them.

"Are you coming to the meeting?" Rachel asked.

"I might," said Danny.

"I'm no good at acting," said Stephen, "but I wouldn't mind doing something practical. Build something, perhaps."

"You must come along, then," said Rachel. "Practical people are very important. Mrs Palgrave said so. Why didn't you turn up earlier? You know you can go to the front of the queue if you've got a priority."

Stephen shrugged. "Didn't really think of it."

"You coming, Matt?" asked Rachel.

Matt turned slightly pink at the thought and shook his head. "Not on your life," he said.

"Go on," said Danny. "Might be a laugh. Hey, didn't we wind Mr Ambrose up about the rubber!"

"Stupid man," said Rachel. "Ugh, he's horrible. He's so fussed about the way his pens fit in his pocket and little tiny things like that, he makes me feel all yukky. Come on, we don't want to be late."

"It's only half-past twelve," said Matt, cutting his scotch egg in half and spearing a chip. "There's heaps of time."

"Oh," said Rachel restlessly. "Yes, I suppose there is."

"And what was all that about Marcia?" asked Stephen.

Matt told him all about it and then, as soon as Sue had finished her cherry yoghurt, Rachel said again, "Come on. It's nicer in the Drama hall than here, even if we are early. See you there, Danny. And Stephen. And you might as well come along, too, Matt."

Matt shook his head firmly. "You lot can make twits of yourselves if you like," he said. "But count me out."

Rachel and Sue pushed open the double doors of the Drama hall and went in. The lights were off and the hall, built without windows, was in semi-darkness. Rachel ran up the steps at the side of the stage and switched on the overhead working light. Then she jumped up and down on the resounding boards. "Oh, isn't it lovely! she cried, holding up her arms. "It's got such a wonderful smell, somehow!" She advanced to the edge of the stage and said, "Can you hear me at the back?"

There was silence in the auditorium and Rachel said, "Sue? Can you hear me?"

"I'm not at the back," said Sue, who had stayed where she was, just inside the door.

"Well, somebody is," said Rachel, peering up at the dark figure sitting silently in the back row. Sue flicked down the switches by the door and the auditorium sprang into light. Rachel sagged when she saw who the solitary watcher was. "I might have known," she said.

"Couldn't hear a word," called Marcia Mudd. "You'll

have to do better than that if you think *you're* getting a part—*dear.*"

"When did you have your lunch?" asked Sue, making her way up the centre aisle to join Marcia.

"Brought sarnies," said Marcia, indicating her orange bag. "Eat 'em when you like, see. All this blasted queueing up and being pushed around gives me the sick."

Mrs Palgrave came in through the door, clipboard in hand. She wore a khaki flying suit with the trousers tucked into black Russian boots, and her fair hair was tied back in a pony tail. "Oh, good," she said briskly. "We've got a few keen spirits! Marcia and Sue. Lovely. Rachel, come off the stage, please."

Rachel put her hand on the edge of the stage and vaulted down.

"You want to try for Cinders, don't you?" said Mrs Palgrave, making a note on her clipboard.

"Yes, please!" said Rachel entreatingly.

"What about you, Marcia?" called Mrs Palgrave. "Cinders, too? You're a bit tall for Cinders, actually."

"No, thanks," Marcia answered clearly from the back of the hall. "I'm not the pathetic sort!" Rachel noticed with annoyance how effortlessly Marcia's voice carried, and how, on this occasion, the beastly girl was managing to speak with no trace of her usual London accent.

"How about the Fairy Godmother?" asked Mrs Palgrave.

"What I'd really like," said Marcia, "would be to have a bash at the Principal Boy. I've done a fair bit of dancing and I can sing."

"Legs?" enquired Mrs Palgrave.

"Smashing!" said Marcia with a grin.

"Right," said Mrs Palgrave, scribbling. "I'll put you on my list for Prince Charming. Sue?"

"Oh, not me," said Sue hastily.

"She'd like to prompt, really," Rachel told Mrs Palgrave. "Only she's too shy to say so."

"Really? Will you be the prompter, Sue?" Mrs Palgrave asked eagerly. "It's always difficult to get anyone reliable. You must come to all the rehearsals, though. I know you'll have the book, but there's nothing so awful as being prompted when you're just having a dramatic pause. You need to know the pace of the thing, you see."

"Yes," said Sue.

Other people had started to drift in, and Mrs Palgrave asked everyone to sit down along the front rows. Miss Duffy had turned up as well, and so had Mr Ellis, the PE master, and Mr Potter, and Mr Fox, who did Woodwork. Mr Pebblemarsh was leaning gloomily against the wall, and Mrs Bath who taught Needlework and always wore rather strange clothes of her own creation, came in looking like the Jack of Diamonds in a tabard embroidered with large slabs of red felt.

"What I want to do today," said Mrs Palgrave, "is allocate everyone to the part they'd like to try for. We'll cast the main parts first, so if you get disappointed for Cinders, say, or for the Fairy Godmother, there's nothing to stop you putting your name down for something else."

"Like a rat," said Rachel gloomily.

"Before we do that," Mrs Palgrave went on, "is there anyone here who is on the technical side? Anyone interested in making or painting scenery, go and see Mr Fox and Mr Pebblemarsh over there by the door. Costumes—see Mrs Bath."

Stephen and a few others started across to Mr Fox, and Roger Smart said, "What if you're interested in lighting?"

"That's my department, too," said Mr Fox.

After some shuffling about, Mr Pebblemarsh said, "We'll take our crew up to the Art room, Norah—er, Mrs Palgrave. Any latecomers, can you shove them up there?"

"OK," said Mrs Palgrave. "Thanks." When the door had shut she went on, "Now, the first two parts I'm going to audition for are Cinders and Prince Charming, because both of these are parts that should be filled from the school, I think. Some of the others might be cast from the staff or parents, so we'll audition for those on Saturday. I'll be sending out a notice. But anyone interested in Cinders and the Prince, come up here."

She handed each girl a photocopied sheet and said, "This

may not be part of our actual production—it's just some words I've written for audition purposes. Go and study them and I'll call you in turn in a minute. Now, anyone here for Buttons?"

"What's that?" asked Danny.

"He's the funny man," John Beasley told him. "I wouldn't mind having a go at that. I saw this panto once and these men were papering a wall and—"

"Yes, we know, John," said Mrs Palgrave. "But I'll put your name down. You, too, Danny."

"What!" said Danny. "Every time we have Drama I'm always a dog, miss."

"Mustn't get typecast," said Mrs Palgrave.

When everyone was organised and all the names were on her list, Mrs Palgrave clapped her hands for silence. "Right!" she said. "Let's have the first candidate for Cinders, then. Pat Allen."

Rachel expected to be first, as she knew her name was first on the list, but she was quite glad to watch someone else before her turn came. Pat Allen was a dumpy fifth year girl with a monotonous voice and Rachel did not fear much opposition from her.

"Here I sit," began Pat, "all alone by the fire while my stepmother and those two dreadful sisters have gone to the Ball." She stood completely still in the middle of the stage, and Rachel made a mental note to establish an imaginary fire to sit by.

"Thank you," said Mrs Palgrave when Pat had finished. "Next—Hannah Beaumont."

Hannah was a different kettle of fish. She had long red hair which she wore pinned rather untidily on top of her head so that wisps escaped and fell either side of her face, and she looked the part completely. But, to Rachel's relief, her voice was thin and did not carry to the back of the hall.

"Sue," she whispered. "*Can* I be heard at the back, do you think? Marcia said—"

"Of course you can," said Sue. "They could probably hear you in Tavenham."

"Oh, good," said Rachel, relieved.

The next candidate was obviously too big for the part although she had a strong voice, and the next one sounded plummy. Wendy James, who followed, looked promising. Her hair was as fair as Mrs Palgrave's, falling in long wisps from a centre parting. Her face was thin and she was very small. Everything she did was neat and precise and she spoke her lines carefully. However, her high-pitched voice had the same fault as Hannah's and everyone had to listen attentively to hear what she was saying. Rachel's heart sank. Wendy was really quite good if she could be persuaded to speak up a bit—and time was going by. The bell would go for afternoon school at any minute, and Rachel had not been heard. Wendy finished her performance and left the stage demurely.

"Rachel Greenberg," called Mrs Palgrave.

Rachel's heart seemed to be pounding so fast that she felt breathless. Deep breaths, she told herself, and don't gabble. She walked up the steps to the stage, took a chair and placed it to one side then sat down on it. She held out her hands to the smoky, cheerless fire which her imagination had conjured up. After so many repetitions she was sure she knew the short passage well enough to do without the script. She dropped her hands disconsolately in her lap, tucked her feet under her chair as if wearing a long, ragged skirt, and began, "Here I sit, all alone by the fire . . ."

Sue and the others clapped loyally when she finished, and Mrs Palgrave held her pencil up in reproof. She glanced at her watch and said, "We haven't time to start on the Princes today but we'll meet again tomorrow, in here at the same time. I won't decide finally on Cinders until I've cast the Prince because they've got to match well together. I can't put a big Cinders with a little Prince."

The bell rang and everyone made their way out.

"I can't bear it," said Rachel, clutching her forehead dramatically. "The suspense is killing me. I just can't *live* until tomorrow."

"In that case," said Mrs Palgrave, "I'd better cross you off the list. I can't have a corpse as Cinders."

Rachel's knees sagged and Sue grinned at her stricken friend. "Serves you right for making such a fuss," she said.

"OTT," said Marcia, shouldering her way out.

"Huh?" enquired Rachel.

Marcia looked back. "Over The Top, you twit. What they used to call Ham. Overdoing it. Call yourself an actress—you don't know nothing, do you?"

And she went out, letting the door swing back in Rachel's furious face.

CHAPTER 6

Auditions

Mr Watts was standing at his desk ominously as they all trooped in to his lesson after lunch. Sensing trouble, everyone sat down very quietly. Mr Watts leaned forward, placing his knuckles on the desk top. With his straight, dark-suited arms and hunched shoulders, he looked like an angry crow.

"Marcia Mudd!" he snapped.

"Yes?" said Marcia.

"Come here."

Marcia flounced down the gangway between the desks and stood in front of Mr Watts.

"I told you to report here first thing this morning," said Mr Watts. "Where were you?"

"Never heard nothing about it," said Marcia innocently. Several people who had given her the message with some glee at registration that morning gasped with indignation, but Mr Watts took no notice.

"You appear to have a perverted sense of humour," he went on. "And what is more, you evidently have no sense at all of the value of property these days. Anyone who will tie a pair of PE shoes recklessly to the back of someone's car is a complete idiot."

"I did what?" asked Marcia.

Mr Watts thumped his desk with his fist. "Don't play the little innocent with me!" he shouted. "Your shoes were tied to my rear bumper, as you well know. And furthermore, they were accompanied by an extremely impertinent note."

"Well, it's got nothing to do with me," said Marcia firmly, "so it's no good you going on about it. Have you got my shoes?"

Mr Watts stared at her, dumbfounded. "I *beg* your pardon?" he asked sarcastically.

Unabashed, Marcia repeated, "Have you got my shoes? I been looking for them all over the place, ever since someone pinched them yesterday."

"I see," said Mr Watts. He stood back from his desk and pushed his hands into his jacket pockets. "It appears," he continued, "that you have been placed in an extremely unpleasant group of people."

"'Sright," agreed Marcia, nodding. She was not wearing earrings today.

"Be quiet!" Mr Watts shouted at her. "I am not inviting your comments! And for all I know, you may be no better. All of you appear to be thieves and liars, totally devoid of the most basic human decency. Go and sit down."

Marcia did as she was told, but turned to say again, "Can I have my shoes back, sir?"

"Williams," snapped Mr Watts, his eye falling on Danny, who was sitting in the front row. "Go and knock on the staff room door and ask for the shoes that Mr Watts found. Where's your tie, boy?"

"Holding my trousers up, sir," said Danny, indicating the tie, which was knotted round his waist.

"Disgusting," said Mr Watts. "Well, go on, boy—hurry up!"

"Yes, sir," said Danny smartly.

Hurrying dutifully along the corridor, he thought with a kind of admiration about Mr Watts's flow of words. It might be quite nice to be a teacher and tell people off like that. "You horrible little boy," he said aloud experimentally. "You scruffy muck-heap. What a nasty, snivelling little beast you are!" It sounded rather impressive. Danny thrust his hands into his pockets in the manner of Mr Watts and went on more loudly, "Your parents should be ashamed of producing something like you, totally unable to think and lacking in all human decency. Where's your tie, boy?" He thought for a moment. "Your brain is as soggy as a wet sponge. *You revolting person*," he declaimed at top volume, shaking his fist, "*You waste of space, you mindless twit*, you GIBBERING IDIOT, YOU—"

Suddenly he heard laughter behind him and turned round

to see Mrs Palgrave carrying a stack of books in one arm. "Danny Williams!" she said, grinning. "What on earth are you on about?"

"Er—I was doing a Mr Watts, miss," said Danny, turning pink with embarrassment.

"Between you and me," said Mrs Palgrave, falling into step beside Danny, "it's a pretty good imitation. I think we'll put a classroom scene in the pantomime—it would bring the house down. But where are you off to? Why are you out of your class?"

"I've got to get Marcia Mudd's shoes from the staff room," Danny told her. "Mr Watts said."

"Yes, I heard about the shoes on the bumper," said Mrs Palgrave thoughtfully. "Who did it, do you know?"

"No, miss," Danny lied, turning even pinker.

Mrs Palgrave looked at him. "I see," she said. "Why has everyone taken such a dislike to Marcia? She seems OK to me."

"She's all right," said Danny cautiously. He liked Mrs Palgrave, but teachers were teachers and there was no telling what they might decide to do if they were told too much.

"M'm," said Mrs Palgrave. "I'd like to know what's going on. Still, it'll sort itself out in time, I suppose."

They came to the staff room door and she added, "I'll get those shoes for you."

"Thank you," said Danny.

The audition for the part of Principal Boy was held at lunch time the following day, and even Rachel had to admit that Marcia was obviously better than anyone else. Several of the girls who did ballet and tap at the Doreen Shaw Dancing School had put their names down to try for Prince Charming, but Marcia was the only contender who had the kind of swagger and dash which the part needed. Helen Oldham, who was the star pupil at Doreen Shaw's, moved very well and had a clear, ringing voice but she was a small, trim girl—too small, Rachel realised with alarm, to be teamed with herself if she should be chosen as Cinders.

After the last girl had done her test piece, Mrs Palgrave

walked on to the stage with her clipboard in her hand and looked out into the auditorium expectantly. An instant silence fell.

"I think you will all agree," she said, "that Marcia Mudd is an outstandingly promising Principal Boy. Although she is a junior, she's tall enough for the part and she has a very good presence on the stage, so I would like to offer her the part. Marcia?"

"Thank you," said Marcia from the hall.

"The part of Cinders was more difficult to decide on," Mrs Palgrave continued. Rachel clasped her hands together in an agony of suspense. "Nobody has exactly the right natural balance of looks and ability. Wendy has a great advantage in looking the part so well, and so has Hannah, although she has a very quiet voice. Rachel—very good acting ability but I hadn't quite imagined Cinders with short, curly hair."

"Wig?" suggested Rachel in a small, anxious voice.

Mrs Palgrave smiled. "Neither had I seen her as someone with quite Rachel's energy," she went on. "However, on balance, I have decided to give Rachel the part, with Wendy as understudy."

Rachel gasped, collapsing on Sue with relief.

"Helen, will you understudy the part of the Prince, please?" asked Mrs Palgrave.

Helen looked sulky. "Does that prevent me from trying for another part?" she asked.

"No, of course not," said Mrs Palgrave. "As long as it's nothing too major—just in case."

"Oh, all right," said Helen reluctantly.

Rachel was beaming broadly. Mrs Palgrave looked at her and said, "I'd like a word with you afterwards, Rachel, please."

Rachel nodded happily.

"Tomorrow evening," Mrs Palgrave went on, "is the meeting for anyone interested in the pantomime in any way. You've all had your notice to take home, but please will you point out to your parents that we need all kinds of help, not just actors. We need people to help with make-up, we need people to sell programmes and provide refreshments, we need carpenters and electricians, and lots of volunteer drivers to fetch and carry things and give people lifts. So do please make sure your mums and dads understand about that. *Any* kind of help is welcome."

The bell rang but Mrs Palgrave held up her hand to keep everyone sitting down. "I'd like to hear people for the part of Buttons tomorrow," she said. "It's a very strong comedy part for a boy—or it could be a man. If there's time, I'll try people for the Fairy Godmother as well. Right, off you go now."

Rachel went to the edge of the stage and looked up at Mrs Palgrave, who said, "Come up here for a minute." Rachel climbed up and followed Mrs Palgrave to the offstage area where the long hessian curtains which formed the wings screened them from anyone else's view.

"Now, look," said Mrs Palgrave. "We've got to get this straight now, otherwise it'll wreck the show. One of the reasons I hesitated about casting you is a doubt about putting you and Marcia together. Now, are you going to be able to work with her?"

For a moment, Rachel did not answer. It was a fair question and one which had been nagging at the back of her own mind.

"You see," Mrs Palgrave went on. "To be honest, it would be easier to find another Cinders than another Prince. The Boy is always a difficult part to cast because so many girls tend to think it's unfeminine. But if putting you two together is going to cause trouble, I'd rather know now."

"It'll be all right," said Rachel. "Honest. I've been trying my best to make friends but—I mean, she's only been here a few days and none of us know her properly yet."

"Are you sure?" persisted Mrs Palgrave. "There's a lot depending on it, you know."

"My part depends on it, for a start," said Rachel ruefully. "So it's *got* to be all right, hasn't it?"

"To put it bluntly," said Mrs Palgrave, "yes, it has. Now run along or you'll be late for registration. Give Mr Potter my apologies and tell him I kept you."

"OK," said Rachel. "Thanks."

"Oh, and Rachel—" Rachel turned and looked questioning. "I think you'll make a very good Cinders," said Mrs Palgrave.

"Thanks!" said Rachel again. She clattered down the steps at the side of the stage, but her smile faded as she went. Acting with Marcia was not going to be easy.

Mr Pebblemarsh and his gangs of what he called "dogsbodies" had been busy. The narrow corridor which led from the Drama hall to the PE changing rooms was completely covered with black paper so that it looked like a dark tunnel. The screens, which consisted of two supports rather like jumping stands bearing a rectangle of perforated hardboard between them, had been placed at angles to the wall and they, too, were covered with black paper so that there was no longer a clear view along the "tunnel". It already began to look quite creepy. Rachel threaded her way between the screens, having decided that it was quicker to go back to Mr Potter's room this way than by the more orthodox route along the covered walk and through the English department. A creeping sense of gloom was beginning to weigh down her spirits, and in the middle of the dark maze she came to a halt, overwhelmed by depression. She had so much wanted to get the part of Cinders but it seemed now that there was no pleasure in having achieved it. Standing alone in the near-darkness, she wondered whether to go to Mrs Palgrave and tell her she could not play the part. But then Marcia would say Rachel had given it up because she was unwilling to act with Marcia. There seemed to be no way out of the situation. Thinking about it unhappily, Rachel ran her fingers over the surface of the screen beside her feeling the regular rows of holes in the perforated hardboard under the black paper. It was, she mused, like being in a dream world, quite apart from the normal reality of school.

Suddenly, as if from nowhere, a figure was close behind her. It seemed to have come out of the wall. Rachel screamed.

"Oh! Good gracious, Rachel, you gave me a fright!" said the figure, which, Rachel realised, was Miss Duffy, the PE mistress. "What on earth are you doing here?

"Where did you come from? gasped Rachel. "I didn't see you."

"I was in the PE store cupboard," said Miss Duffy, indicating the black-papered wall behind her. "Checking hockey balls." She turned, inserted a key into the lock, which was almost invisible in its black surround, and clicked it shut.

"I'd forgotten—that there was a cupboard," said Rachel, breathless with shock.

"Well, there is," said Miss Duffy rather crossly. "And I think it's high time you were somewhere else." Being on her way to take a Dance lesson, she wore a leotard and tights, and she whisked away through the maze of screens as neatly as a rather indignant cat. Or perhaps, Rachel thought, glaring after her, she was more like a newt. Slim and somehow wriggly. All she needed was a tail.

Annoyance overcame her alarm. Why had the silly woman come bouncing out of the cupboard like that? She ought to look where she was going. Rachel made her way back to Mr Potter's classroom, only to find the others already on their way to History.

"There you are!" said Sue. "I brought your books." She handed Rachel her airline bag.

"Thanks a lot," said Rachel gratefully. "Did you tell Mr Potter I was here?"

"Yes, we said you were talking to Mrs Palgrave," said Debbie. "He was ever so pleased to have two of his class in the pantomime."

"Well, I'm glad *somebody's* pleased," said Rachel.

Quite a lot of people turned up the following evening for the meeting about the pantomime. They occupied at least the first ten rows of seats in the Drama hall. On the stage, sitting behind a long trestle table, were Mr Hazzard, Mrs Palgrave, wearing her Russian boots with a peasant skirt and a black sweater, and all the other teachers concerned with the pantomime, including Mrs Gipsum, who taught Music and had turned up attired in a tight blue dress which made her look even fatter then usual. Mrs Bath was there too, wearing a kind of tent made of crochet, tied round the waist with a multi-thonged leather belt with lots of wooden beads on it.

"What a strange lady," said Rachel's mother. "She looks like an ethnic shopping bag."

"Shut up," said Rachel. "That's Mrs Bath."

"Who's the fat blue one?"

"Mrs Gipsum. Teaches Music."

"Heavens," said Mrs Greenberg. "Do you like her?"

Rachel hesitated. "She gives concerts," she said, "so she must be good at music. But she's so boring."

"Perhaps she finds school boring," said Rachel's mother.

"Perhaps," agreed Rachel. She waved at Sue, who had just come in with her mother, and craned her neck to see who else she could see. "There's Danny," she said. "That small boy with untidy hair. With the woman in the pink cardigan. I wonder if that little fat man is Danny's father? He's not as untidy as Danny."

"Perhaps he grew out of it," said her mother. "Is Danny going to be in the pantomime?"

"He might be Buttons," said Rachel. "Unless Mrs Palgrave finds someone better among the grown-ups. He was ever so funny at the audition this lunch time, doing a sketch about a teacher with a class of bank managers. And Judith Ellistone's going to be the Fairy Godmother. She's in the sixth form." Rachel could see no sign of Matt or Stephen, but Debbie and Felicity were sitting together with their parents, and John Beasley had arrived with his father, a huge man in a checked sport jacket and a mauve polo-necked sweater.

Then Marcia came through the door, arm in arm with a curly-haired man in white corduroy trousers and a buff open-necked shirt with a scarf tucked into it. Over this he wore a short brown waistcoat, unbuttoned.

"Who's *that*?" asked Rachel's mother.

"It's the dreaded Marcia," said Rachel. "And the man must be her dad. I've only seen him once before, if that's who it is, and then he was wearing jeans and a donkey jacket."

To Rachel's annoyance, her mother watched with interest as Marcia and her father came up the aisle between the rows of seats and sat down some distance behind them.

"Does she come to school looking like that?" Mrs Greenberg asked.

"More or less," said Rachel. "Isn't she *awful*!"

"I don't know," said her mother. "She might be all right, underneath the mad exterior. At least she's not dull."

"M'm," said Rachel evasively. To her relief, Mr Hazzard got to his feet. As he did so, the stage lights, which were being used this evening instead of the working light, were brought up by an invisible hand to a multicoloured radiance. Rachel giggled. "He ought to sing a song," she whispered.

Mr Hazzard made a short speech of welcome and introduced the teachers who sat on the stage with him, ending with Mrs Palgrave, who then got up to speak in her turn.

"In a minute," she said, "when my colleagues have explained exactly what it is that each of them do and what kind of help they need in their particular department, we're each going to set up our own recruiting shop, so to speak, so that you can come and talk directly to the person concerned. For my sins, I'm producing the show, so I'll be here on the stage to talk to aspiring actors." She went on to outline the parts that needed to be filled and said there would be auditions the following morning—a Saturday—and on Tuesday evening and the Saturday of next week. "By that time," she ended, "the thing has simply *got* to be cast. Now, before I hand you over to Mr Fox, are there any questions?"

Nobody said anything, but Mr Potter looked up and remarked, "Just in case anyone's wondering, we haven't finished writing the show yet, although several of us are hard at it. So if anyone's got any bright ideas about what to put in, we'd like to hear from you."

A rather severe-looking woman sitting in the front of the hall got up and said, "Mr Headmaster, would it not make more educational sense to complete the writing of the 'show' as you call it, before attempting to find the actors?"

"Er—" began Mr Hazzard. But he was interrupted by a man's voice ringing out from the back of the hall. "I'd like to say a word about that, if I may?"

All heads turned. Marcia's father was on his feet.

The Headmaster nodded. "Of course, Mr—"

"Mudd," said Marcia's father. "May as well get that over, for a start-off. My name is Mudd. Alwayss good for a laugh." There was a polite smile from the rest of the audience. "No," Mr Mudd went on. "What I want to say is, I hand it to this school for the way they're really trying to involve the kids. And their parents and everybody. Most schools you go to, they dish out some old play with cobwebs on it, the kids learn their lines and that's that. So I'd say to the lady at the front, whoever she is, before she starts laying down the law about what's educational and what isn't, she just wants to think about it." He sat down.

Several people clapped and Mr Potter called, "Thank you!" but there were mutters of disapproval and the woman at the front got to her feet again. Mr Hazzard stood up. "I am delighted to have so much interest shown, but I'm afraid we can't turn this into a general debate at the moment or we'll never get anything done. I'll ask Mr Fox to speak to you now about the technical side of things, then Mrs Bath and Miss Duffy would like a word, and after that we'll stop for some well-earned refreshments." He smiled and sat down.

"This Mr Mudd sounds quite a character," whispered Rachel's mother. "I must meet him at coffee time."

Rachel nodded thoughtfully. "So must I," she said.

Mr Pebblemarsh appealed for help on the technical side. "Anyone who can knock a nail in straight is welcome," he said, adding gloomily, "or even crooked. Who are we to fuss? Mr Fox will welcome you with open arms. And we need a gang of ladies with sewing machines, and if you've ever done painting-by-numbers, here's where you can try painting-by-Pebblemarsh—same sort of thing, but bigger." He went on about scenery painting for a while, then sat down. Mrs Gipsum, blinking vaguely, said that anyone with musical talent was welcome to come and see her about a part in the pantomime but she was sure the main attraction would be the impressive display of musical ability within the school.

Mr Potter cast a slightly reproving glance at Mrs Gipsum as he got up. "The main point is," he explained, "we want this pantomime to include absolutely everyone who'd like a finger in the pie, from the Chairman of Governors to the smallest first year in the school."

"He must mean Danny!" Rachel whispered.

"This year," Mr Potter went on, "we've deliberately chosen a pantomime rather than a straight play so as to give the younger ones a chance. Last year's production of T S Eliot's 'Murder in the Cathedral' was very much a sixth form effort, and we're keen to enlist support this time from further down the school. In fact, we always find the older boys a bit reluctant to get up on a stage—perhaps they think it's unmanly. All I can say is, wait until they've seen Mr Pebblemarsh in a ballet skirt." When the laughter died down he added, "We're proposing to run this pantomime for five performances during the next-to-last week of term, starting on the Tuesday night and including a matinée on the Saturday. We have written to all the local business firms we can think of, hoping they will place an advertisement in the programme to help defray expenses, but if you know of anyone else who might welcome the enormous publicity we can offer, do please tell us!"

A fat woman sitting in the hall got up to say she could offer them a pale blue leotard to fit a child aged eight, and a man said he used to do a clog dance when he was younger. "Yes," said Mr Potter, slightly wall-eyed. "Well, after our break I'm sure the appropriate people will be delighted to deal with these offers. Now I propose that we adjourn to the sixth form common room at the rear of this hall for coffee, supplied by Miss Banbury and some of the girls from her Home Economics department."

Everyone got up and within a few minutes the sixth form common room was jammed with people.

"Those biscuits look nice," said Rachel. "Home-made. Only two pence each."

"Help yourself," said her mother, giving her a pound note. "And pay for my coffee, there's a dear. I'm going to see Mr Mudd." She made her way purposefully across the room.

Sue arrived with her mother. "Hello," she said to Rachel. "You know my mum, don't you?"

Rachel nodded. "Hello, Mrs Eames," she said.

"Hello, dear," said Mrs Eames.

"'Scuse me a minute," said Rachel. "I *must* go and see someone." She gave Sue a huge wink and a jerk of the head in Marcia's direction, and added to the girl serving coffee, "Back in a minute. I'm not running off without paying."

"Better not," said the girl.

Sue, after some gazing round, had perceived what Rachel meant and said, "Oh, so must I. See you in a minute, Mum."

"All right, dear," said Mrs Eames peacefully.

Rachel's mother was shaking hands with Mr Mudd. "Call me Harry," he said. "Everyone else does."

"My name's Alice," said Rachel's mother. "Oh, and here's my daughter Rachel."

"And Rachel's friend Sue," said Rachel. "Hello!"

"Hello," said Harry. "Have you met Marcia? She's only been in the school two minutes but she's got the lead part in the show. Great, isn't it?" He smiled at Marcia, who stood by his side, drinking a cup of coffee.

"Great," said Rachel enthusiastically. "Yes, we know Marcia. She's in our class." Then she added with the same enthusiasm, "She was telling us what a wonderful house you've got."

"Oh, was she?" asked Harry guardedly.

"Yes, all about the gold taps and the sunken bath and how it's miles out in the country so you don't have visitors," said Rachel. She sounded immensely impressed, but her mother looked at her suspiciously and Marcia shot her a glance of pure hatred.

"We don't do too badly," said Harry.

"I do agree with you about what's education and what isn't," said Alice Greenberg, changing the subject firmly. "Most schools are so narrow-minded."

"Well, they never managed to teach me much at school," said Harry cheerfully.

"You done all right, though," said Marcia.

"We get by, don't we?" said her father, smiling at her.

"Where exactly *do* you live?" Sue asked baldly.

Harry looked at her. Then he gave her a wink and a knowing shake of the head. "Like Marcia says, miles from anywhere," he said.

"Why don't you two go and play?" enquired Alice Greenberg, staring at Rachel and Sue.

"Sorry," said Rachel at once. "Come on, Sue, they'll have sold all the biscuits." She smiled at Harry nicely and added, "Lovely to have met you. See you on Monday, Marcia."

"Yeah," said Marcia.

Rachel headed back towards the table where Sue's mother was still standing. "But I only wanted to *know*," protested Sue at her heels. Rachel glanced back at her friend impatiently. "You're such a twit," she said. "That was just one question too many."

CHAPTER 7

The Horror Run

"My mum's going to be in the pantomime," said Danny on the bus on Monday morning.

"Is she?" Matt sounded surprised. "I didn't know she was good at acting."

"She says she used to like it at school," said Danny. "She came to the meeting on Saturday morning, and Mrs Palgrave said she could be the Princess who was going to marry the Prince before Cinders came along."

"I suppose she's small enough," said Matt thoughtfully. "She can't be any taller than Marcia. Perhaps that's why you're such a shrimp."

"And I'm definitely going to be Buttons," Danny went on, ignoring this insult.

"What do you have to do?" asked Matt.

"There's some dancing," said Danny, "and a sketch about a school and I don't know what else yet. He's called Buttons because the uniform has buttons all the way down the front."

"What uniform?" asked Matt, confused.

"A boy that works in a posh hotel or somewhere. Carrying suitcases upstairs and polishing shoes. Pages, they call them. A bit like Mr Pebblemarsh's dogsbodies."

"Oh," said Matt. "I see. What a load of rubbish."

Rachel leaned across and said, "Was Marcia's dad there?"

"Oh, yes," said Danny. "He was quite funny. Mrs Palgrave wants him to be the Stepmother."

"Oh, great," said Rachel bitterly. "Talk about being stuck in the Mudds! I'll be surrounded by them."

"I quite like him, really," said Danny. "Why weren't you there on Saturday, Rachel? You ought to have come."

"I couldn't," said Rachel. "I go to Drama classes at Miss Pettit's on Saturday mornings. I'm doing my LAMDA exams with her, you see, and the next one is quite soon. I explained to Mrs Palgrave and she said she didn't mind. When the exam's over I'll be able to come on Saturdays."

"It won't matter much," said Danny. "Mrs Palgrave says she can rehearse the children and the grown-ups separately for a while, until we have to put it all together. Everyone has their own bit, you see, rather like variety turns, she says. So we can do our bits during school time, and the grown-ups can do theirs at weekends and after school."

"I think Mrs Palgrave is wonderful," said Rachel. "Fancy doing all that."

"I still want to be a horse," said Felicity.

"Me, too," agreed Debbie. "We can both be a horse. I don't mind being the back legs."

"You'd better tell Mr Potter, then," advised Rachel. "Make sure he writes a part for you."

There was a pause.

"Did you ever find out where Marcia lives?" asked Stephen. "I mean, *is* she at Prospect Row?"

"Huh!" said Sue, who obviously still felt this to be a sore point.

"No," admitted Rachel. "We had a bit of a failure about that. And my mother said it was very rude to ask people questions about their personal circumstances. She gave me an awful telling-off after the meeting on Friday night."

"Why?" asked Stephen.

Rachel explained.

"Well," said Sue. "I did try. Anyway," she added more cheerfully. "This Hallowe'en thing sounds fun. I hope they'll have pumpkin lanterns and things."

"When is it?" asked Danny.

"Next Friday night," said Sue. "It's on that list of dates they gave us at the beginning of term, but I expect they'll send a reminder notice out this week."

"Bound to," said Matt. "They're always sending out notices about one thing or another, aren't they? No wonder Mr Hazzard says the school has a big paper bill."

"Better than doing nothing," said Rachel. "Here, Matt—you know Ollie Withett, the assistant caretaker?"

"Yes," said Matt cautiously. "Why?"

"Well, you know how he looks a bit like an apeman, with all that black hair and thick eyebrows and long arms—wouldn't he be marvellous as an Ugly Sister!"

"Oh, terrific!" said Danny. "Why don't you ask him, Matt—you know him better than we do."

"Not really," said Matt. "He came to my house once, that's all."

"Do ask him, Matt," said Rachel.

"I suppose I could," said Matt. "But I bet he won't."

When the bus arrived at school, Ollie was poking about with a spiked stick under the bushes retrieving crisps bags and of bits of paper.

"Hello," said Matt, approaching.

Ollie scraped off a spikeful of papers into his bucket and said, "I hate crisps bags."

"We think you ought to be in the pantomime," said Matt. "Mrs Palgrave wants everyone to be in it. And we thought you'd be great."

"It's enough of a blooming pantomime round here without that," said Ollie.

Matt helpfully retrieved a crumpled paper bag and put it in Ollie's bucket. "I didn't think you'd want to," he said.

"Dead right," said Ollie.

The rest of the week went past amazingly quickly. Mr Potter rushed about with untidy sheaves of paper clutched in his arms, and there were great sounds of hammering and sawing from the workshops as Mr Fox and his helpers set about the construction of scenery. Mr Pebblemarsh's dogsbodies worked on an endless output of ghastly figures for the Horror Run, arriving in the Art room at every spare moment. Matt was among these, for he liked Mr Pebblemarsh and had always enjoyed painting—and it made a change from listening to Rachel and the other members of the cast eternally discussing the pantomime.

"All it takes is a sniff of greasepaint," said Mr Pebblemarsh gloomily, "and all these girls are throwing temperament like prima donnas. Mugs like us never get our name in lights."

"Don't want to," said Matt stoutly. He was filling in the black-outlined ribs of a skeleton with fluorescent paint.

"Oh, I'd quite like it," said Mr Pebblemarsh, "But I gave that idea up when I realised there isn't a theatre in England wide enough for my name. Benjamin Pebblemarsh—I mean, if they were going to get it all in, the letters would only be a few centimetres high. They could shorten it to BP, I suppose, but then I'd look like a petrol station."

"Can't win," said Matt.

"Not a hope," agreed Mr Pebblemarsh. He stared round at the other workers. "Oy!" he said, pouncing on two girls who were painting a ghost. "It's too pretty. We'll never scare 'em stiff that way. Your ghost looks as if it's wearing a Dorothy Perkins nightie. Next thing we'll have lace and rosebuds. Horror, we want! Rotting flesh and clutching hands and blood dripping from the fingernails."

"Nasty," said one of the girls distastefully. "When we do the scenery for the pantomime, sir, can we make it pretty?"

"Oh, Lord, yes," said Mr Pebblemarsh. "All sweetness and light, laid on with a trowel."

"I think horror's great," said Matt, whose face was streaked with paint.

"Much more fun," agreed Stephen.

Mr Pebblemarsh looked thoughtful. "I might turn this project over to you boys," he said. "You can run the whole thing. Then me and the girls can get cracking on the panto."

Stephen saluted smartly. "You can trust us, sir," he said.

"Absolutely," agreed Matt.

"Great!" said Mr Pebblemarsh. "But you'll have to keep at it. Deadline this Friday. Hurry-hurry. Horror-horror." He wandered off with his eyes bulging more dementedly than ever.

Rachel and Sue came to see what Matt was up to.

"It looks marvellous!" said Sue. "Ever so creepy. What's all this raffia with beads on the end?"

"It's going to hang from the ceiling so it brushes against people's faces as they go through," Matt told them. "And we're going to have wet sponges so you put your hand on them unexpectedly and—"

"That'll do!" shouted Mr Pebblemarsh from the other side of the room. "Don't tell the customers all about it, Matt, or you'll spoil the surprise. You'd better go and get your dinner now, or they'll shut up shop."

Matt washed his brushes and took off his overall.

"I got such a fright when Miss Duffy came out of that cupboard," said Rachel. "I screamed my head off. I didn't mean to, but I just did."

"I bet Marcia wouldn't have screamed," said Sue. "I don't think *anything* could frighten her."

"She'd be just as scared as I was," said Rachel, nettled. "In fact," she added thoughtfully, "I think that's just what she needs."

They were walking along the corridor towards the dining area. Sue looked at her friend in perplexity and said, "What do you mean?"

Rachel thought for a minute before replying. Then she said, "Well, we've got to do something about Marcia. I admit I don't like her, but if I'm going to keep my part in the pantomime, I've *got* to like her. Or at least, get on with her."

"What's that got to do with giving her a fright!" asked Matt.

"It's a bit difficult to explain," said Rachel. "But I think the reason why she annoys me so much is the way nothing ever upsets her. She's so cool and superior, she gives you the feeling she can't be got at."

"Except the time Matt said he didn't believe her dad was rich," Sue reminded her.

"That's what I mean," said Rachel. "I bet she's not as cool as she seems. If we'd had a real old row the day Matt upset her it might have cleared the air. As it is, nobody says anything at all except little snide remarks."

"So what do you want to do?" asked Matt.

"If only we could give her some kind of really awful fright," said Rachel. "Like Miss Duffy gave me, only worse. Nothing dangerous, but just very scaring. It might make her forget to be superior for a minute. And while she's all shaken up, we might be able to talk to her—get her to be more reasonable.

Even if it means having a row. Anything would be better than going on the way we are now."

"It sounds a bit dodgy to me," said Matt. "She *is* a pain in the neck, though."

"We ought to rescue her," said Sue romantically. "If she was shut in a dungeon or something, and we came and let her out, she'd be so grateful she'd be our friend for ever."

"Dungeon!" snorted Matt. "You do talk rubbish, Sue."

But Rachel was standing stock-still, her face alight with excitement. "That's it!" she said. "Brilliant!"

"Oh, come on, Rachel," said Matt. "There'll be no dinner left."

"There's always sausage rolls and things," said Rachel, but quickening her pace a little. "I know what we'll do. Miss Duffy came out of the cupboard, right? Well, Marcia can go *into* the cupboard. It's going to be dark, isn't it, Matt?"

"The Horror Run? Oh, yes, pitch," said Matt.

"Good. And will there be noises—groaning and clanking chains and things?"

"Yes," said Matt cautiously. "But I can't tell you—"

"Oh, don't be silly, Matt! I'm not going to spoil your precious surprise! All I want to know is whether there'll be plenty of noise going on. Because if we shove her into the PE cupboard, a bit of extra screaming isn't going to matter."

"You can't do that!" said Matt, scandalised. Then he grinned. "Or can you?"

"Why not?" asked Rachel.

Sue beamed. "Of course we can!" she said. "And in a little while we can go and let her out and be really nice to her."

"Not unless she's good and frightened," said Rachel.

"It won't work," said Matt. "To start with, the cupboard's locked."

They arrived at the serving hatch and found the dinner ladies clearing up the trays of food.

"Oh, are we too late!" Rachel asked pathetically. "We've been helping Mr Pebblemarsh and we're ever so hungry."

"Oh, dear," said the lady. "We've got some meat pie left, if you'd like that. And beans."

"That would be fine," said Matt.

"And chips?" asked Rachel hopefully.

"Chips are all finished, dear. There's mash."

Rachel hesitated. "OK," she said heroically. "Mash."

As she ate her dinner—without mashed potatoes—Sue pondered on Rachel's idea. The thought of rescuing a distraught Marcia from a dark prison was a very attractive one. Marcia was so superior, and looked at Sue with such contempt, that it would be very satisfactory to have the positions reversed. And besides—Sue had to admit to herself that there was something about Marcia which she found intriguing. She would very much like to know her better, even if the means of doing so threatened to be unorthodox or even alarming.

"Couldn't we get the key to that cupboard?" she said.

Rachel thought deeply. "Tricky," she said. "Do the cupboards each have their own key, or is there one that opens all of them?"

"Mr Pebblemarsh has got a key that opens everything," said Matt, who had also been thinking. "He says he can never remember which is which, so he just uses one."

"Where does he keep it?" asked Sue.

"On a nail inside his stock cupboard door," said Matt.

"That's it!" said Rachel. "Problem solved. We get Marcia to go through the Horror Run on her own, have the cupboard ready unlocked and station a couple of people beside it. When she comes along, they push her into it and lock it."

"She'll know who they were," objected Sue.

"No, she won't," said Rachel. "At least, I hope she won't. If it's dark in there, like Matt says, anyone going in from outside won't be able to see a thing until their eyes get used to it. People who've been in there some time will be OK."

"Actually," said Matt a little reluctantly, "we're going to have two or three people dressed all in black, with awful masks, leaping about and frightening people."

Rachel spread her hands and smiled. "There we are, then," she said. "Next time you see Mr Pebblemarsh, Matt, tell him he's got an extra frightener."

"Who?" asked Sue

"Me," said Rachel.

On Friday night the school presented an unusual appearance. A hidden spotlight among the bushes picked out a twice-lifesize skeleton dangling outside the Drama hall, and grinning pumpkin lamps glowed in every dark window. As Rachel walked across the car park with her parents, screams and giggles could be heard coming from the buildings.

"I bet it's not usually like this," said Mr Greenberg.

"Too right!" agreed Rachel. Out of the corner of her eye she noticed the Rolls Royce standing among the other cars.

"Look at that!" exclaimed her father. "Who's the millionaire around here?"

"Harry Mudd," said Rachel.

"He's the man I was telling you about," Alice Greenberg explained to her husband. "Lots of charm but could be a con man. Rachel's doubtful about the gold taps."

"Well, the Rolls is solid enough," said Rachel's father.

They went into the foyer, where Mr Hazzard, dressed in an academic gown with silver cardboard stars pinned on to it, smiled and said, "Good evening."

"Hello, Mr Hazzard," said Rachel's mother. "You've met my husband, haven't you?"

"Yes, indeed," said Mr Hazzard, shaking hands.

"I've got to go and help Mr Pebblemarsh," said Rachel. "See you later."

She escaped, leaving her parents talking to the Headmaster. The only visitors who had arrived so far were those whose children had something to do with running the Hallowe'en night, but even so, the school was already quite crowded. Mrs Gipsum had selected suitable music for the occasion and "The Sorcerer's Apprentice" was booming through the Tannoy.

Rachel was wearing black tights and her black PE leotard under her sweater and jeans, and she had borrowed a full-sleeved black blouse from her mother on the vague grounds that it was needed for the pantomime.

Arriving in the Art room, she found Mr Pebblemarsh sitting on a table, eating a sandwich, while three black-clad figures cavorted round the room in hideous masks.

"Felicity?" said Rachel.

One of the figures pranced up and said, "Oh, *there* you are! We've been ready for ages. Come and get changed."

"Where?" asked Rachel.

"In my stock cupboard," said Mr Pebblemarsh gloomily. "That's why I'm exiled out here."

In the stock cupboard, Felicity discarded her mask as Rachel peeled off her jeans and sweater.

"Who are the other two?" asked Rachel.

"Peter Box and Michael Chalmers," said Felicity. "They're standing by to push!"

"She won't know what hit her," said Rachel, buttoning up the voluminous blouse.

Felicity laughed, then asked, "Why are you wearing that blouse? You'd be all right just in your leotard."

"I've got such skinny arms, she might recognise me," said Rachel. "With this on, nobody would know who I was."

"You're right there," agreed Felicity. "That's the key, look. The thin-looking one with a label saying Master."

"As opposed to Mistress?" Rachel wondered.

"Don't be daft," said Felicity. "It means it's a master key that opens everything."

"Joke," explained Rachel.

"Oh," said Felicity.

Rachel put her mask on. "We'd better take the key now," she said, her voice muffled behind the rows of yellow fangs. "Just in case he locks this cupboard up or something."

"He never locks anything until he goes home," Felicity assured her. She glanced round the cluttered stock cupboard and added, "He really does need tidying up, actually. We'll have to take him in hand one day."

"Not me," said Rachel from inside the mask. "I *hate* clearing up. Ready, then?"

Felicity picked up her mask and then said, "Wait a minute. How are we going to make sure Marcia will come into the Run?"

"I've left that to Stephen," said Rachel. "Sue offered, but she might giggle. Stephen will be OK."

Mr Pebblemarsh appeared at the door. "Come on, ladies," he said. "We'll have customers arriving any minute now."

"Just coming," said Rachel. "Oh—can you fix my mask, Mr Pebblemarsh? There's a bit of wire sticking out and it's making a groove in my chin."

As she went out with Mr Pebblemarsh, she pointed a black-clad arm behind her at the key which hung on the door. Felicity took it down, folded it inside the cardboard label which was tied to it, and slipped it up the tight-fitting sleeve of her leotard.

CHAPTER 8

"It's All Gone Wrong"

Sue was looking for Stephen. She had been very much offended by Rachel's assumption that Stephen was the only person capable of persuading Marcia to venture through the Horror Run alone, and the school was so crowded with strangers tonight that there was every chance that Marcia's downfall would happen without Sue being involved in it at all. And she was determined not to be left out.

Matt, taking five pences at the Horror Run, shook his head when Sue approached. "Not a sign of her yet," he said. Sue went to look elsewhere, threading her way between the groups of giggling girls who screamed delightedly at Mr Pebblemarsh's spooky figures which hung everywhere. The boys did not scream, but added to the general feeling of pleasant hysteria by pretending to be ghosts and uttering a variety of moans and howls.

Stephen was not at Miss Banbury's gingerbread stall. He was not at Mr Fox's Blowing Out the Candles competition, nor was he at the Apple Bobbing, where apples hung on strings, or the Apple Ducking, where apples floated in a tin bath full of water. He was not at the home-made coffee stall, or Mrs Palgrave's Support The Pantomime stall, or at Mr Murdoch's Trial of Strength, which consisted of trying to hammer a long nail into a log. Sue began to despair.

"What's the matter, Susan?" asked Mr Hazzard kindly as Sue crossed the foyer on her way to the Drama hall corridor. "You look very worried. Lost your mum and dad?"

"They're not here tonight," said Sue. "They had to go to something at Dad's office. His boss is retiring."

"Oh, I see," said Mr Hazzard.

"I was looking for Stephen Chuff, actually," said Sue. "Or Marcia."

"I've just seen both of them," said Mr Hazzard. "They went through to the Drama hall with Mr Mudd and the Greenbergs. It's nice to see that Marcia's making friends."

"Yes," said Sue. "Thank you, sir." She hurried through the door that led to the covered walk and so round to the Drama hall. Of course, that's where they would go. Marcia was interested in nothing but the pantomime, and Mrs Bath's sketches for the costumes were on show in the Drama hall. Sue pushed open the swing doors. There were quite a few people in the Drama hall, craning their necks to gaze at the sloping roof with its looped cables and lighting battens, and the tiered seats with bold white letters on the floor of each row. Stephen and the others were standing by a pin-board where Mrs Bath's designs were displayed.

Sue went over to them. "Hello," she said, suddenly feeling very shy.

"Oh, hello, Sue," said Mrs Greenberg. Marcia nodded without enthusiasm and her father said, "We met you on Friday night, didn't we?"

"Yes," said Sue, blushing. She knew he hadn't forgotten her rash question about where he lived. Still, she told herself, any ordinary person wouldn't mind being asked.

"They're good drawings, aren't they?" she said.

"Smashing," said Harry Mudd. "Marcia's going to look a treat in that lot." He indicated the sketch of a figure jauntily attired in tights and high-heeled boots, a closely-buckled jacket and a hat with a fly-away feather in it.

"Lovely," agreed Sue. There was a pause, and, for something to say, she said, "You're helping with the set, aren't you, Stephen?"

"Yes," said Stephen. "Back-room boy, me. Hammer and nails." He grinned and added, "Acting's all right for girls, but when it comes to real work, it takes us men to do it."

"Cobblers," said Marcia, rising to the bait. "We can do whatever we want."

"That's my girl," said Harry proudly.

Stephen shook his head. "They're the weaker sex, aren't they?" he said. "I mean, you're scared of spiders, Sue."

"*I'm* not," said Marcia.

"And Rachel's always saying she's not afraid of anything," Stephen went on. "But look what happened when Miss Duffy startled her in the Horror Run the other day. Screamed the place down—and there was nothing there except black paper! Nothing scary about it."

"I bet it's scary now," said Sue with a little shiver. She and Stephen exchanged a glance of secret understanding and he said determindedly, "I don't care what anyone says—girls scream when they go through the Horror Run, and boys don't. So boys are tougher than girls."

"What is this Horror Run?" asked Harry Mudd.

"Oh, it's just a stupid collection of stuff the Art teacher put together," said Marcia scornfully. "Paintings of skeletons and that. Don't know what there is to scream at."

"Bet *you'd* scream," said Sue, hoping she was saying the right thing this time.

"'Course she would," agreed Stephen.

"I'll show you," said Marcia. "Come on, Dad."

"Rachel was on her own," said Sue quickly. "It wouldn't be frightening if your parents were with you."

"Well, Rachel's certainly got over her nerves now," said Alice Greenberg in her daughter's defence. "She was off up there like a shot this evening, helping Mr Pebblemarsh."

Sue glanced at Stephen in alarm. Did Rachel's mother know that Rachel was one of the black-clad figures? Was she going to tell Marcia? But it was Marcia herself who unintentionally avoided the danger. "Go and get some of that gingerbread you said you fancied," she said to her father. "Takes more than a few silly paintings to scare me. See you at the gingerbread place in a minute, right?"

"Right," agreed her father readily. "You don't want us old fogies about, anyway. Better on your own with your mates. You got enough money?"

"Yes, thanks," said Marcia. She set off for the door, and as Sue followed her with Stephen, she heard Harry saying to the Greenbergs, "It's great to see her making friends. Coming to a new area like this . . ." His voice faded as the door swung to beind them.

"Hello," said Matt as they came to the Horror Run. "Have

you come for a scare, Marcia?" He spoke rather loudly, partly because of the screams and groans and clankings which came from the darkened corridor behind him and partly, Sue realised, to warn the people inside that Marcia was on her way.

"Marcia has," Sue said with emphasis. "I'll come afterwards—just to make sure she hasn't died of fright." She hoped they had heard her. She didn't want to be the one to end up in the black cupboard.

"Huh!" said Marcia, fishing in her purse for five pence. "Fancy being scared of all that rubbish." She put the coin in the box on the table in front of Matt. Then she turned to Stephen. "You coming?" she asked.

"No," said Stephen. "Got no money."

"I'll pay for you if you want," said Marcia.

Sue caught Matt's eye and the same thought flashed between them. Was Marcia just a little scared, after all?

Stephen grinned. "Want me to hold your hand, do you?" he asked. It was the last straw.

"Oh, shove off," said Marcia. With a toss of her unnaturally bright red hair, she walked past them into the shrieking, groaning darkness.

"Good luck, Marcia!" Sue shouted after her. And a burst of manic laughter came in response from the blackness.

"That sounds like Rachel," said Matt, grinning. "Go in and see if they've done it, Sue."

"Me?" Despite her rash promise to follow Marcia, Sue felt a lurch of alarm. "I mean—they haven't had time yet," she added quickly.

"Go on," said Stephen. "It'll take you a few minutes to get used to the darkness. I'd better not come because I told her I wouldn't. If she happened to see me she might smell a rat."

"Oh—well, all right," said Sue relunctantly.

"You're not *scared*, are you?" asked Stephen. "You know it's only us."

"'Course I'm not scared," said Sue stoutly.

"I'm going up to the Art room," said Stephen. "I don't want Old Man Mudd to catch me here if he comes looking for

Madam. See you there, Sue—you can come up the stairs from the other side of the Run."

Sue swallowed hard. "Right," she said. There was nothing for it. She walked past the first screen into the darkness, trying hard not to think of spiders.

A dim light flicked on, showing up one of Matt's paintings of a fiend with dripping fingernails, and a fluorescent skeleton glowed in the blackness. As she turned to grope her way forward there was a shriek of laughter and she found herself pushing through strands of something which clung to her face and hair. It's not spider's web, she told herself resolutely. It's just raffia and stuff. Matt said. Treading blindly over a thick mat, her foot pressed something below it which emitted a doleful blaring noise—and at that moment an invisible hand pushed her shoulder. Sue gasped. A flickering light picked out a hideous mask right in front of her, with scarlet-rimmed eyes and jagged yellow teeth. "It's me," said the mask in Rachel's voice. "We've done it!"

"Oh, good," said Sue rather shakily. "I'd better get up to the Art room and tell Stephen."

"Right," said Rachel. And, with a gleeful shriek, she leapt away into the darkness.

Sue blundered on, trying not to look at the dancing skeletons and shielding her face from the creeping, dangling things which touched her. Groping ahead of her, she put her hand on something horribly wet and soft which she did not immediately recognise as a wall of damp sponges. Stifling a shriek, she felt her way round another screen—and came face to face with a huge, hairy spider. She screamed. Another mask loomed up beside her and Peter Box said, "Don't be daft. It's only a painting. Marcia did it."

Sue was angry as well as shaken when she emerged into the daylight. It was ironic, she thought, that it should be Marcia's painting which had scared her—almost as though Marcia was having her own back. Still feeling rather shaky, she ran upstairs to the Art room. Stephen was there, looking at the blackboard on which there was a notice in Mr Pebblemarsh's angular writing. It said, "Gone for coffee. *Has anybody seen my key?* BP"

"Oh, dear," said Sue. "There's going to be trouble."

"No, there isn't," said Stephen. "We'll go and get the key and put it in his desk drawer or something."

"Or in his overall pocket," suggested Sue, pointing at the brown warehouse coat which Mr Pebblemarsh usually wore and which now lay across his chair.

"The only trouble is," said Stephen, frowning, "we'll have to borrow it again to let her out. And you can't expect BP to think he's lost it *again*—not twice in one evening."

"Come on," said Sue, moving towards the door. "Let's go and let her out now."

Stephen shook his head. "No, thanks. I don't want to be around when she comes out of there, and neither do you. We're the ones who persuaded her to go in, and if we're the ones who let her out—"

"We're the ones who get the blame," Sue finished. "But we must do something before Mr Pebblemarsh gets back."

"I'll go and see what Rachel thinks," said Stephen. "You stay here. Do some tidying up or something in case BP comes in. Look natural."

He went out, and Sue rather half-heartedly went over to the sink and turned on the tap. There was a clutter of wet paste brushes lying in some dirty water, and she gathered them into a bunch and held their clogged bristles under the tap. Art was a horrid subject, she thought; messy and somehow vague. There were never any right answers in Art. There weren't even any questions, so how could you start to get it right? She envied the people like Matt, who seemed to understand it without even trying. She finished the paste brushes and picked up a wet piece of rag which had once been part of someone's pyjamas but was now sodden and dirty brown with assorted spilt paint. Distastefully, she dropped it back on the draining board. She wandered along the bench, replacing the lids on the tins of powder colour. If there was a dustpan and brush, she thought, she wouldn't mind sweeping up the spilt powder. But there wasn't—and nothing would induce her to use that disgusting rag.

Mr Pebblemarsh came in. "Hello, Sue!" he said, surprised. "Whatever are you doing here?"

"I just came to see if Rachel was about," said Sue. "And she wasn't, so—"

"You've been clearing up!" said Mr Pebblemarsh, coming over to the bench. "I'm amazed! No, that really is very nice, Sue, thanks a lot. We must have a blitz once all this Hallowe-en business is over, and get the place really tidied up."

Out of the corner of her eye, Sue saw Stephen come in. He nodded at her and held up the key. Then he went across to where Mr Pebblemarsh's overall lay across his chair.

"Shall I put these paste brushes in a jar or something?" asked Sue.

"Yes, stick them in a jam jar, bristles up," said Mr Pebblemarsh. "And if you're feeling really energetic, there's a cloth over by the sink—"

"Actually, I must go and find Rachel's parents," said Sue quickly, "and make sure they'll give me a lift home. My dad dropped me here, you see, but he and Mum had to—"

"Have you found your key yet, sir?" asked Stephen, coming over.

"No, I haven't," said Mr Pebblemarsh, scratching his beard in a worried sort of way. "It's a bit odd, that. I'm pretty sure it was on the nail behind the door. If someone's nicked it I'm in dead trouble because it opens everything. I'll have to report it to the Head, and all the locks will have to be changed and Lord knows what. And it makes me look a right Charlie."

"Perhaps you had it in your pocket," Sue suggested.

"I don't think anyone would pinch it," Stephen assured him.

Mr Pebblemarsh shook his head. "I wish I shared your faith in human nature," he said.

"But you do," Sue pointed out. "Otherwise you wouldn't leave your key where people can take it."

"True," said Mr Pebblemarsh. "The trouble with me is, I'm a mug."

Then he looked sharply towards the door as an extra-ordinary noise came to their ears—a mixture of sobbing and screaming and voices raised in loud argument.

"What on earth's going on?" asked Mr Pebblemarsh.

Sue and Stephen rushed to the door. The rumpus was coming from the bottom of the staircase. Stephen ran down the steps, closely followed by Sue and Mr Pebblemarsh.

Felicity, who had removed her mask, and Rachel, who had not, were grappling with Marcia, who was sobbing and screaming.

"You rotten sods!" she shrieked. "I hate this blasted school! I wish I'd never come here! Her red hair was dishevelled, and her face was swollen with crying and streaked with the mascara which had run down her cheeks.

"You were only in there for about five minutes!" shouted Felicity, who was trying to urge Marcia away from the crowd of visitors who were staring in consternation at the scene. The masked figures of Peter Box and Michael Chalmers hovered uneasily in the background.

"Get your hands off me!" yelled Marcia. "How would you like it, shut up in a little black hole? I can't bear being shut up—I can't *stand* it!"

"Come on up to the Art room, love," said Mr Pebblemarsh soothingly, trying to put his arm round the hysterical girl's shoulders.

"Get off!" screamed Marcia. "Don't you touch me!" She gave Mr Pebblemarsh a violent push which made him stagger back for a moment, tore herself away from Felicity's restraining arm and fled through the swing doors of the Drama hall with Sue and the others at her heels.

Marcia ran past the front of the stage and out of the other door, still sobbing loudly. She rushed across the covered area and through the door into the English department, down the corridor and into the foyer. To Sue's immense relief, Mr Hazzard was no longer there—but Mrs Abbott stood at the far side of the foyer talking to some parents.

"Dad!" screamed Marcia. "Where's my dad?"

Harry Mudd had just come through the door at the other side of the foyer, chatting amiably to the Greenbergs and carrying several bulging paper bags and two toffee apples. His face changed to utter consternation as his daughter hurled herself at him.

"We gotta go home," she sobbed. "I'm not stopping in this

place no more. Come on, Dad. COME ON!" Her voice rose to a shriek, and Mrs Abbott hurried across the foyer to intervene.

"What on earth is going on?" she demanded. "Marcia, control yourself at once!"

"Shut up!" shouted Marcia.

Her father put his arm round her shoulders as she buried her face in his jacket. He glared at the other children. "What you lot been up to?" he demanded. He stared at Rachel, who still wore her yellow-fanged mask, and added, "Who's that?"

Rachel took her mask off and Harry said, "Oh. Little Miss Clever-boots. What you been doing to Marcia?"

"I'm sure Rachel wouldn't—" began Mrs Greenberg.

"Oh, *wouldn't* she?" snarled Harry.

"Will you please stop this noise at once!" shouted Mrs Abbott.

"Don't you tell me to shut up!" shouted Harry. Marcia tore herself away from his embrace and ran across the foyer to the door which led out to the car park.

"I really must insist on an explanation," said Mrs Abbott.

"Are you coming?" Marcia yelled at Harry. He started after her, clutching his rather squashed paper bags to his chest, and pushed open the door with his free hand, which still held two toffee apples. Marcia had disappeared into the darkness outside. Mrs Abbott ran after Harry angrily and was rash enough to make a grab at his coat sleeve. "Mr Mudd!" she demanded. "I do insist—"

Harry turned. "What you got to insist about?" he shouted. "If anyone's got explaining to do, *you* have! So leave me alone and keep your bloody kids in order!"

"Oh!" spluttered Mrs Abbott, outraged.

But the Mudds had gone. In a few moments the sweeping beam of the Rolls Royce's headlights swung across the car park as the huge car drove away at speed.

"Well," said Mr Pebblemarsh. "What do we do now?"

Nobody answered. The door opened again and Danny came in, untidy as ever. "The Mudds were in a hurry," he remarked cheerfully. Then he looked from face to face and added, "Have I missed something?"

"You've missed everything," muttered Rachel, who dared not smile.

"I think you'd better come home," her mother said to her. "I want to know what's been going on."

"If you don't mind, Mrs Greenberg," said Mrs Abbott tightly, "I would like to speak to all these people before they go anywhere."

"We're supposed to be in the Horror Run," said Peter.

"What's happened?" asked Danny, looking bewildered.

"None of us know," Mr Greenberg told him.

"I think everybody had better come back to my Art room," said Mr Pebblemarsh gloomily.

Mrs Bath, wearing a white satin shift and a headband with an ostrich feather in it, walked across the foyer talking to Mrs Gipsum, and Mrs Abbott ran across to intercept them. "Will you ask Mr Hazzard to come up to the Art room," she said. "Urgently."

Everyone trooped back through the English department and across the covered way into the Drama hall, and from there up the stairs to the Art room.

"It all went wrong," said Rachel to Sue, who was walking beside her ahead of Stephen and Felicity and Danny. "Why did Stephen decide to unlock the door so soon? I wanted to talk to her and I never got a chance."

"He had to," Sue explained. "Mr Pebblemarsh had noticed that his key had gone. Did she just come bursting out, or what?"

"No," said Rachel. "Stephen took the key from Felicity and put it in the door and turned it, and nothing happened. We listened, but there was such a lot of noise going on with the tape-recorded screaming and everything, we couldn't hear anything from inside. So he just took the key out of the lock and went off with it. And some more people came into the Run, so I had to go and do my shrieking and moaning bit, and when I was doing it I heard Felicity shout, 'Marcia, wait a minute!' I suppose Marcia had found that the door was open and just come bursting out like you said. I tried to stop her, but she was like a mad thing."

"She certainly was," said Sue. "Didn't she find the light switch? Was she shut up there in the dark?"

"It's behind the boxes of hockey balls," said Rachel. "I had a job finding it when I went for some bean bags."

Sue shook her head. "I wish we hadn't done it," she said.

"I still think it was a good idea," said Rachel obstinately. "It's a pity tonight is a Friday—we'll have to wait until Monday before we see her. But we'll just have to talk to her then. You never know, it may still be all right, once she's calmed down."

"I think it's going to be terrible," said Sue with foreboding.

As they all went into the Art room, Mrs Abbott looked at the chalked notice on the blackboard and said, "Mr *Pebblemarsh*! Am I to understand that you have lost a master key?"

"Er—no," said Mr Pebblemarsh, flustered. "I found it. I mean—it's about." He cleaned the board hastily and said, dusting his hands with a certain desperation, "Do sit down and make yourselves at home. Sorry it's a bit of a tip in here."

He pulled out a couple of stools for his unexpected guests and whisked his overall off the back of his chair.

"There's your key, sir!" said Stephen, pointing at the chair seat. "It must have fallen out of your pocket."

"Careless," said Mrs Abbott heavily. "Keys should be kept in a place of security at all times."

"Yes," said Mr Pebblemarsh meekly. "Quite right." He took the key into his stock cupboard, giving Stephen the ghost of a wink as he went.

"Now," said Mrs Abbott, folding her arms. "I want a precise account of what has happened tonight. Let me see—who is the least likely to make up any silly stories?" Her gaze flicked from face to face and came to rest on Sue. "Susan Eames," she decided. "*You* tell me."

Sue gulped, and cast a distraught glance at Rachel, who shrugged. Mr Hazzard had arrived and stood listening in the doorway. "Well," Sue began. "It was like this . . ."

CHAPTER 9

In the Café

Marcia was not at school on Monday.

"I'm ashamed of you lot," said Mr Potter as he totalled the register and closed it. "And Mr Hazzard is absolutely disgusted. I thought you were all pretty nice people and now what do I find? You've been hounding a girl who is new to the school, teasing her and persecuting her until this morning she's not here because she can't face it any more."

"She might just have a cold," objected Rachel.

Mr Potter stared at her severely. "Just for once in your life," he said, "you might have the decency to keep your opinions to yourself, Rachel. I know all about what happened on Friday night and I've little doubt that you were at the bottom of it."

Rachel folded her arms and stared offendedly out of the window, but Sue, glancing at her friend, saw the tell-tale patches of colour on her cheeks and knew that Mr Potter's words had struck home.

"I know Marcia isn't the easiest person in the world to get on with," Mr Potter went on. "But she's had a pretty difficult life of it, and I think you might be a bit more understanding."

Matt put his hand up cautiously.

"Yes, Matt?" said Mr Potter.

"You can't be understanding if you don't know what there is to understand, sir," said Matt. "I mean, Rachel said all along that what we want to do is *talk* to Marcia—but we can't. I mean, she doesn't want to talk, and we don't know what she's so stroppy about."

Mr Potter looked at him consideringly. "I can see what you mean," he admitted. "But if one has confidential information about someone, it has to remain confidential."

"What's he on about?" John Bleasley muttered to Peter Box, who said, "No idea."

"What I mean," said Mr Potter, "is that *you* wouldn't like it if I knew something private about you—something you wouldn't like generally known—and then you found out I'd been rabbiting on about it to everyone."

"Say what you like about me," said John comfortably. "No skin off my nose."

"That's all very well for you!" Felicity told him indignantly. "Someone else might have some awful secret that really worried them." She turned to Mr Potter. "If it's something like that with Marcia, sir, couldn't you tell us? It would make things much better."

"I can't," said Mr Potter flatly. "No teacher could."

"Well, then," said Rachel waspishly. "If you won't explain, you can't blame us for not understanding, can you?"

"You don't *have* to understand," said Mr Potter firmly. "Just behave like decent human beings, that's all."

"That's what Mr Hazzard said on Friday night," said Stephen.

Rachel rolled her eyes reminiscently. "What *didn't* he say!" she remarked.

Marcia was not at school the next day, or the next. As time went by with no sign of her return, Mrs Palgrave began to get worried.

"Does anyone know what's happening about Marcia?" she demanded at a lunch time rehearsal. "We're all very worried about her, but if she isn't coming back soon, Helen will have to take over the part."

"We don't know," said Rachel, looking anxious. Helen Oldham was smaller than Marcia, and Rachel was very much aware that Helen, with her short, dark hair and slight frame, would look much better teamed with Rachel's blond understudy, Wendy, than she would with Rachel herself.

"We may have to re-think the whole thing," said Mrs Palgrave, frowning. "I knew it was a mistake to put you two together."

"Honestly, Mrs Palgrave," said Rachel earnestly. "I know

it's hard to believe, but I really was trying to be helpful."

"Well, you picked a funny way to do it," retorted Mrs Palgrave. "Now, who have we got who *is* reliable? Danny—come on, I've got the complete script for your bit with the Fairy Godmother now."

"Oh, dear," lamented Sue, who was turning up faithfully to every rehearsal. "This term looked like being such fun and now it's gone all wrong."

The next day Marcia was still not at school.

"This is getting serious," said Mr Potter as he closed the register. He glared round at the class. "I hope you realise you're in pretty big trouble. You've probably done a great of deal of damage, not just to Marcia and her family, but to the school's reputation."

There was an uneasy silence. It was almost time for the bell to go. Matt put up his hand.

"What is it?" snapped Mr Potter.

"Nothing, sir—I mean, I've got a note to say I'm going to the dentist," said Matt.

"Oh. What time?"

"Three o'clock, sir."

"Leave about half-past two, then," said Mr Potter. "Keep your note for whoever teaches you then. *Did I say you could talk*?" he added fiercely to the rest of the class.

Rachel sighed. But even she did not dare to make any comment.

Matt did not like going to the dentist but he consoled himself with the thought that he would miss half Mrs Abbott's History lesson. As the minute hand crept round to twenty-five past two he put up his hand. Mrs Abbott nodded impatiently and said, "Go along, then. Quietly."

Mr Bell was a cheerful dentist and although he had a habit of asking questions which could not be answered when he had half his hand and various tools inside the patient's mouth, Matt quite liked him. And besides, when Mr Bell let him out of the front door with a bright smile and a wave of farewell, Matt found himself in the enviable position of being legitimately out of school. At half-past three, there was no point in going back. He could catch a bus straight home from the bus station in Flaxton.

Matt plodded past the brightly-lit shop windows in the November afternoon. After the warmth of the dentist' surgery, the air felt raw and cold, and when he consulted the timetable he found that he had twenty minutes to wait before the bus left. There was a small café across the road whose steamy windows looked inviting. A cup of coffee, Matt thought, would fill in the next twenty minutes very pleasantly. He made his way across the road and pushed open the door.

"Yes?" said the man behind the counter.

"Coffee, please," said Matt.

"Like to sit down, I'll bring it," said the man, indicating an empty seat with a nod of his head. The café was crowded with bus drivers and conductors and intending passengers.

Matt moved towards the place the man had indicated, then stopped. The other half of the bench seat was occupied by Marcia Mudd.

"Hello, Fred," said Marcia calmly, moving her orange bag closer to her to make room for Matt. "What you doing out?"

"Been to the dentist," said Matt.

"I thought you might have been skiving," said Marcia, "but you're one of the good sort, aren't you. Well, sit down, then," she added impatiently. "Don't stand there staring."

Matt sat down cautiously. "I thought you were ill," he said. "Or something."

"Well, I am ill, aren't I?" said Marcia crossly. "Off me flaming head. Having a nervous breakdown. That's what I told the social worker, anyway."

"Social worker?"

"Yeah. Always someone coming round to mind your business for you. Must have been Mr Hazzard sent her, I reckon. She was round Saturday morning—didn't lose much time, did she?"

"No," said Matt, embarrassed. The man brought his coffee and said, "Pay at the till," and went back behind the counter.

Matt stirred the coffee, sipped it and put the cup back in the saucer. "Look," he said bravely. "I'm sorry about Friday night. That business about the cupboard."

Marcia shrugged. "Just the bloomin' end, innit?" she said. "I suppose I went over the top a bit, but if there's one thing I can't stand, it's being shut up. Never could. A woman shut me in a tool shed once, and I smashed all the windows. That was the end of another lovely foster home. Anyway, I'm not going back to Mill Green no more. Schools are all the same. People say they're your friends, but they're not. Everyone mucks you about."

"Have you been to a lot of schools?" asked Matt.

"Yeah," said Marcia indifferently, then repeated, "they're all the same."

"What does your dad say? Doesn't he mind you being away?"

Marcia looked at Matt for a minute without replying. Then she said, "He thinks I'm going to school. Him and that social worker went on and on about how it was my last chance, and I thought, well, rather than have him all upset." She scowled. "And don't you dare let on!"

"No, of course not," said Matt. "It's nothing to do with me, anyway." Then he frowned. "But—do you stay out all day, then? Where do you go?"

"Leave the house in the morning, right time," said Marcia. "Walk into town, hang round the shops for a bit, go in the park if it's fine."

"But I thought your dad brought you to school," said Matt, thinking of the Rolls Royce.

Marcia shook her head and the jazzy red hair tumbled forward over her dark eyebrows. "No," she said. "Just that first day."

"Did you come on the bus after that?" asked Matt.

"Walked," said Marcia.

Matt thought about the long day spent wandering round the streets and sitting in cafés. "Doesn't your dad go to work?" he asked. "I mean, can't you go home?"

Marcia looked at him pityingly. "Neighbours'd let on, wouldn't they?"

Neighbours. Matt remembered the address beside Marcia's name in the register. 19, Prospect Row. There wouldn't be any neighbours if they lived in a big house in the country. And she wouldn't be able to walk to school from there, either. The register must be right.

Marcia's eyes had narrowed into a suspicious stare. "Well, go on, then," she said.

Matt blushed. "What do you mean?"

"You may as well say what you're thinking."

Matt shrugged. He tried to sound casual as he said, "Just this address business. House in the country."

"Yeah," said Marcia. She pushed a few crumbs about on the empty plate before her with a scarlet fingernail, then glanced up at Matt. "Blown it, haven't I?"

"It's all right," said Matt, acutely embarrassed. "I mean, I don't mind one way or the other." He tried to drink his coffee in an unconcerned way but his awareness of Marcia's unwavering gaze made him feel hot and uncomfortable.

"If I tell you," said Marcia suddenly, "will you promise not to tell that girl?"

"Rachel?"

"Yes. She really hates me."

"Oh, I don't think she—"

"Will you promise or not?"

Matt gulped. "Yes," he said. "I promise."

Marcia's black-rimmed eyes narrowed. "You'd better mean that. If I find out you've told her—"

"I won't tell her," said Matt.

Marcia swilled the cold dregs of her coffee once round in its cup then put it back in its saucer. "I live in Prospect Row," she said. "No gold taps. We're lucky to have a bathroom at all. Dad works in a toy factory. Still—" A touch of her bravado returned— "It's Entertainments, innit?"

"Actually," Matt admitted, "it says Prospect Row in the register."

"So they all know?"

"Well—I don't think they quite believed what you said about your cook living there."

"Did I say that?" Marcia gave a husky laugh. "I tell so many lies, I forget what I said."

"But your dad does have a Rolls Royce," said Matt. "Doesn't he?"

"Nah," said Marcia. "Friend of his works for a hire firm, doesn't he? Lets Dad borrow the Roller if he wants to cut a dash."

"But why bother?" asked Matt, puzzled. "You could have said where you really lived. Things like that don't matter."

"Oh, yes, they do," said Marcia grimly. "They do to my dad, anyway. He was inside, you see. Long stretch for GBH."

"What's that?" asked Matt.

"Grevious Bodily Harm. He did a bloke over who was chatting up my mum or something—I don't know much about it. He says he had a hot temper when he was younger. But anyway, Mum went off with another bloke."

Matt nodded. "My dad left home," he said. "But me and Mum are OK. How old were you when that happened?"

"Two," said Marcia. "I can't really remember her. She is an actress, that was right enough, but the sort of films she makes—well, Dad says they're for clubs and that. Know what I mean?"

Matt didn't, but he nodded.

"Anyway, I was in care for a year," Marcia went on. "Most of the time I was in a Home and then I lived with different foster families, never long with the same lot. Can't blame them, really, I did awful things. Then when Dad came out of prison he met Doreen—she's all right, Doreen is—and the Council said he could have me back, and they gave us this house in Prospect Row. It's pretty grotty, but he always says we'll have a mansion one day." She laughed shortly. "Joke."

"But it's all *right*," Matt assured her. "Nobody would mind. Honestly they wouldn't."

"Oh, yes, they would," said Marcia. "You don't know, Fred, you've had it easy. Well, fairly easy. People mind about everything, I reckon. But anyway, when we got this house, Dad said we were going to hold our heads up, good as anyone else. Better, he said. Specially me. He wanted me to be the greatest thing the school had ever seen."

"So that's why he borrowed the Rolls?" asked Matt.

Marcia swilled the cold coffee again, nodding. "Silly, innit?"

Matt sat back, pushing his hands into his pockets. "I can see how he feels," he said. "And I can see why you don't want him to know you're skiving. He'd feel all let down."

"'Sright," said Marcia.

"He's bound to find out," said Matt. "Specially if he's in this pantomime. You can't keep it a secret for ever."

"I won't tell him when the rehearsals are," said Marcia, frowning. "If he doesn't turn up, that Drama teacher will have to pick someone else. Just keep my fingers crossed she doesn't ring up or anything." She thought for a minute, then added, "She wasn't bad as teachers go."

"The school will write to your dad," said Matt. "Asking why you're away."

"Oh, they already have," said Marcia cheerfully. "But the post comes after he's gone out, so I get to it first at half-past four. Doreen's out at the mushroom factory all day. She's a packer."

Matt shook his head in reluctant admiration. Then he looked at his watch. Three minutes to go before the bus. "You know," he said cautiously, "I'm sure Rachel would understand, if you told her. I could explain—"

"Don't you dare!" Marcia pointed the teaspoon at Matt threateningly, and her London accent became more pronounced as she resumed her tough, gangster-girl image. "Now look, Fred, you're the only one as knows. I didn't ought to have told you but—I dunno. I thought you was OK. A nice boy. But if anyone says anything, I'll know it was you told them. And I'll get you for it, so help me."

"Don't be like that," said Matt. "You don't have to worry—I won't tell anyone." He stood up. "I'll have to go. There isn't another bus for an hour."

"See you, then," said Marcia, not moving.

"Are you staying here?" asked Matt.

"Yeah," said Marcia. "For a bit."

"Well—see you."

Marcia raised a hand in a casual gesture of farewell, chin cupped in the palm of the other hand, her elbow on the table among the dirty crockery.

Matt went to the till at the end of the counter and paid for his coffee. Then he put down some more coins and said, "That's for another cup of coffee—for the red-haired girl over there."

Then he went out.

Rachel was complaining loudly on the school bus the next morning. "Why did she make such a fuss?" she said. "She was only in the cupboard for about five minutes. There was no need to go into a permanent sulk about it."

"Perhaps she was very upset," said Matt. "Some people have a thing about confined spaces, don't they? Something—phobia." He wished he could tell Rachel all about it.

"Claustro," said Rachel. "Well, the cupboard isn't all *that* small, and if she hadn't panicked she could have felt her way round the wall until she found the light switch, even if it was behind a box or two. No, I think she's just making the most of it. She knows if she doesn't come back to school the pantomime will be all upset and I'll probably lose my part. She's having her own back."

"Why should you lose your part?" asked Matt rather impatiently. He couldn't help thinking of Marcia, walking about all day with nowhere to go. And this morning it was raining.

"Because the Prince ought to be a bit taller than Cinders, said Rachel, "or at least the same height. Marcia's taller than me, and we look OK together. But Helen's a shrimpy little thing and if *she* plays the Prince she's going to make me look like an elephant. And I bet Mrs Palgrave will take one look and say we'd better have Wendy playing Cinders instead of me, because she's tiny, and all that blonde hair and—"

"I'm sure she won't," put in Sue reassuringly. "You're much better than Wendy. You can't hear her at the back."

"I know," said Rachel morosely. "But I've got this awful feeling about it. Just you wait and see."

Rachel was right. At the lunch time rehearsal Mrs Palgrave said, "Is there any news of Marcia?"

Nobody answered.

"Is anyone in contact with her?" Mrs Palgrave persisted. "Does anyone know what's going on?"

People looked at each other but nobody said anything. Matt, who had only turned up because he had nothing else to do, felt uncomfortable. He could so easily set the record straight, but he could not break his promise to Marcia. It would be such a betrayal.

"In that case," said Mrs Palgrave, "I am going to have to make some changes. Helen and Rachel and Wendy, will you come and see me afterwards, please?"

Rachel buried her face in her hands.

By registration time that afternoon, everyone knew that Rachel had lost her part in the pantomime.

"Cheer up," Matt said to her as she sat, tear-blotched and huddled, behind her desk. "Isn't there some other good part you can have?"

Rachel shook her head.

"It's all cast," Felicity explained. "You can be my half of the horse, Rachel, if you like."

"Don't want to be a blasted horse," said Rachel, and gave a reluctant laugh because it sounded so ludicrous. She blew her nose hard. "Just you wait," she said. "I'm going to murder that girl."

Nobody had to ask which girl she meant.

"What about Marcia's dad?" asked Stephen suddenly. "Is he still going to play the Stepmother?"

"I think so," said Danny. "Mrs Palgrave asked him last Saturday if he'd do it, and he seemed to love the idea. But if Marcia's dropped out of it, perhaps he will, too." Matt opened his mouth to say something, then shut it again. He had almost pointed out that Harry Mudd didn't know Marcia had been away from school, so he wouldn't know that his own role as Stepmother was in doubt.

"We can find out tomorrow," said Debbie. "I expect he'll be at rehearsal—he's turned up every Saturday so far."

"I don't think they're doing his bit tomorrow," said Debbie. "Mrs Palgrave said they're going to start the dance routine for Miss Duffy's men."

"My dad's in that," said John Beasley.

"What?" asked Sue.

"That dancing thing."

Everyone fell about with laughter at the thought of John Beasley's father dancing at all, let alone in a frilly skirt. He was a huge man who normally wore a T-shirt so tight over his bulging arms that it looked as if it was going to burst.

"What if Mr Mudd *doesn't* play the Stepmother?" asked Debbie.

"Mr Potter could do it," suggested Felicity.

"No, Mr Potter's the butler at the palace," Sue reminded her. "He's one of Miss Duffy's dancing men."

"I'm what?" asked Mr Potter, coming in.

"Aren't you one of Miss Duffy's dancing class, sir?" asked Felicity.

"I am, for my sins," admitted Mr Potter.

"Are you going to be at rehearsal tomorrow?" asked Danny with a hopeful gleam in his eye.

Mr Potter ran his fingers through his hair. "Yes," he said.

"Oh, we'll all come and watch!" said Bill North.

"No, you won't," said Mr Potter at once. "All you people who've got nothing to do with the pantomime can jolly well mind your own business. You can have your laugh when we perform it. Until then, we'll make fools of ourselves in private."

"Sir, who'll do the Stepmother if Mr Mudd won't?" asked Rachel, who had recovered a little.

"I've no idea," said Mr Potter. "We'll tackle that problem when it arises—if it does. I very much hope that Marcia will soon be back at school and the whole unpleasant business will be cleared up."

"We thought Ollie would be good," said Danny. "But Matt asked him and he said he wouldn't."

"When you've all quite finished running the show," said Mr Potter coldly, "I'll call the register."

In Science that afternoon, Mr Mount, who had a long face and floppy hair like Matt's, only thinner, said he wanted them to take a sample of how many living creatures there were in the school field.

"Including Mr Ellis?" enquired Stephen, watching the PE master trot out after his group of football-jerseyed boys.

"Not *on* the field," corrected Mr Mount. "In it. We are going to measure out areas exactly a metre square and find out what worms and other creatures live in the earth beneath that square."

"Dig it up, you mean?" asked Bill.

"No," said Mr Mount patiently. "We will bring the creatures to the surface by applying potassium permanganate . . ."

It took some time to get things organised, mostly because nobody was very interested in worms, and partly because Rachel was trying to decide what to do about Marcia.

"She's not going to get away with it," she said to Matt. "Something's got to be done."

"What, though?" asked Matt in some alarm.

"I want teams of four," said Mr Mount loudly, "each one with a measuring tape, a notebook and—"

"I've got to make her come back to school," said Rachel.

"But you can't," objected Matt, even more alarmed. "I mean, you don't even know where she lives."

"You lot over there," shouted Mr Mount. "You are paying no attention at all! Which groups are you in?"

"Me and Sue, Felicity and Deb," said Rachel at once. "And Matt and Danny are with Peter and John." Her eyes remained thoughtfully on Matt's face and she was clearly continuing to mull over the question of Marcia.

"Well, come and get your things," instructed Mr Mount. "And stop talking."

They collected their equipment and drifted out on to the field with the others.

"Actually," said Rachel, "I bet she *does* live at nineteen, Prospect Row. I don't believe that story about the cook."

"You can't be sure," objected Matt feebly. "She said it was out in the country." If Rachel turned up at Prospect Row, Marcia would at once assume that he had told her.

"Country, my foot," said Rachel. "If that's the address in the register, that's where I'm going to look. For a start-off, anyway."

"I don't think you ought to," said Matt, frowning. "It's none of our business."

"Whose side are you on?" asked Rachel, staring at him. "Don't you think I've got a right to try and get my part back?"

"Well—yes," admitted Matt. "But—"

He was relieved when Mr Mount came striding crossly over the grass in his clean green Wellington boots. "Will you people please show some interest!" he demanded. "Biology isn't just sitting in a warm room drawing pretty pictures of flowers, you know. It's a real, living science."

"Yes, sir," said Rachel, smothering a sigh. She unreeled a metre of her carpenter's measure from its metal case and looked at it purposefully, then pushed it back again as Mr Mount went to round up some other stragglers.

"Worms!" she said with contempt. "I've got more important things to think about than worms!"

CHAPTER 10

Dancing—and a Drama

On Saturday morning Sue persuaded her father to drop her at school so that she could attend the rehearsal.

"Can't understand *wanting* to go to school," he grumbled as he drove the car into the bus park at Mill Green. "When I was at school I was supposed to turn up for cross-country running on Saturdays and I was for ever trying to get out of it."

"So would I if it was cross-country running," said Sue. "But this is different."

"Must be," said her faher. "What time shall I pick you up?"

"About twelve?" suggested Sue.

"OK." Her father thought briefly. "Might be a bit later. I've got a few things to do in Flaxton."

"Whenever you like," said Sue politely. "Just come into the Drama hall. It's that building over there."

"Right," said her father. "See you." And he drove away.

There were quite a lot of people in the Drama hall. Mrs Gipsum was playing a Chopin waltz rather slowly, emphasising the rhythm with nods of her head, and Miss Duffy was going through a dance routine on the stage with John Beasley's father, watched by several other grinning men.

"Then in to the centre," she instructed. "Point the toe and touch fingers with your partner—no, don't have your hand like a *shovel*, Mr Beasley—and flit away again to the side of the stage." She flitted. Mr Beasley shuffled. In the back row, Danny and Stephen were leaning on each other, helpless with laughter. Sue went to join them, giggling. "Now, don't forget," Miss Duffy went on seriously, addressing the whole group of men. "All of you, whenever you are in your basic position—that's to say, while the soloist is doing his bit—you must always stand like this." She extended one foot so that the pointed toe just touched the ground and put her hands together, resting her cheek against them poetically. "When you're wearing your little feather headdresses it will look sweet," she said. "And you stay in this position all the time while Mr Potter and Mr Pebblemarsh do their pas de deux in the centre of the stage."

"Oh, 'eck," said Mr Beasley.

"It's really not too difficult," said Miss Duffy. "It's just a question of training the muscles."

"Er—look," said Mr Potter nervously. "Do we have to take this seriously? I mean, it's supposed to be funny, isn't it?"

"Oh, yes," agreed Miss Duffy. "But you see, the nearer you are to the real thing, the funnier it looks when it's not quite right. I don't mind a bit of clumsiness, but the main thing to achieve is the *look* of a dancer. A good dancer always looks into the distance, you see—through the wall, as we say." She demonstrated, her small head beautifully poised. "You see? You must feel as if you are suspended from the ceiling by a hook on the top of your head—your neck must be as long as you can make it. And your eyes look to the distant horizon. You try it, Mr Beasley."

"I think you'd better call me Bert," said Mr Beasley.

"That would be nice," said Miss Duffy, still businesslike. "My name's Jennifer. Now, Bert, have a go at the look."

Bert managed to look as if he had smelt something extremely nasty, and was rewarded with guffaws of laughter from the others.

"A little more remote, if you can manage it," advised Jennifer. "Frank, you try it."

Mr Potter stumped on to the stage and duly gazed.

"I didn't know his name was Frank!" Sue whispered to Danny.

"M'm," said Miss Duffy doubtfully. "Perhaps it would be better if you took your glasses off."

"Can't do that, Jen," said Mr Potter. "I'd crash into everyone."

"Oh. Well, in that case you'll have to keep them on. It'll be quite funny, actually. We'll dress you in the classic ballet costume, you see—black sleeveless tunic over a white blouse with floppy sleeves, and tights, of course. And glasses."

"Lovely," said Mr Potter without enthusiasm. "What's Ben going to wear?"

"Mr Pebblemarsh!" hissed Danny, delighted.

"He's taking the ballerina's part, so he'll be in a tutu," said Miss Duffy.

"What's that?" asked Bert.

"A very short white frilly skirt that sticks straight out from the waist," Miss Duffy explained. "It has a tight-fitting satin bodice, and of course he'll have pale pink tights and pink ballet shoes tied with ribbon."

"I'm not shaving my beard off!" said Mr Pebblemarsh in some alarm at this description.

"Of course not!" Miss Duffy reassured him. "Again, that's what will be funny. We'll have a perfect 'première danceuse'—except that she's rather big and she's got this bushy beard."

"I shall never keep a straight face," said one of the other fathers, a balding man in a dark suit with a striped tie.

"Yes, you will," said Jennifer Duffy firmly. "Now—I've shown you the steps. All come on to the stage and we'll go through it once more and then we'll try it with the piano."

The motley collection of fathers shuffled on to the stage.

"Where's Mrs Palgrave?" asked Sue.

"She's in the sixth form common room with my mum and some of the others," said Danny. "They're going through the lines for the scene in the Palace when the Prince can't find Cinders after the Ball, and the jealous Princess wants to know why he can't marry *her*. That's my mum's part. And she's got a song to do! It's called, 'What's She Got That I Haven't Got?' Mrs Gipsum wrote it."

"*Did* she?" Sue was impressed. "I didn't think she could actually *write* music."

"Some of our teachers are quite clever, really," said Stephen. "There's two sorts, aren't there—the ones that do things and the ones that don't."

"Yes," Sue agreed. "And the ones that do things are the

ones that do everything. You'd never get someone like Mr Ambrose joining in. Or Miss White."

"Or Mrs Abbott," said Stephen.

"She does turn up, though," Danny pointed out.

"Only to boss everyone about after all the work's been done," said Sue. "I wish she'd go off and be a headmistress somewhere."

"She's too old," said Dannv.

"I don't know—the headmistress of our primary school was ancient," said Sue. She laughed. "We all thought she was a witch. We used to tell the little new kids that she kept her broomstick in the cupboard opposite her office. Lots of them believed it."

"Scary things, cupboards," said Stephen.

Sue looked at him. "I do wish we hadn't done it," she said.

"Pushed Marcia in the cupboard?" said Danny. "Yes, perhaps it was a mistake."

"*Well*," said Stephen with contempt. "After all that talk about how nothing scared her, who'd have thought she'd go screaming off like that? I think it's tough on Rachel, losing her part and everything. It's not *her* fault."

"It is in a way," said Sue reluctantly. "I mean, if we hadn't done anything to Marcia, she'd still be here."

"She *might* still be here," corrected Stephen. "With someone as nutty as her, you can't be sure."

Sue had to admit that this was true. "I wonder what Rachel's doing today?" she said. She had a nasty feeling that Rachel was thinking up some drastic plan of action.

"She was saying on the bus she's got an aunt and uncle coming to see them," said Danny.

"Oh, yes!" remembered Sue. "Auntie Miriam. She mentioned it yesterday morning."

"Oh, look!" said Danny, collapsing into giggles again. Miss Duffy's troupe of men were solemnly going through their routine, accompanied by Mrs Gipsum's thumping Chopin waltz.

"*One*—two—three . . . turn *out*—and to the side. No, *little* steps, Bert!" Miss Duffy, Sue thought, was like a circus trainer with a ringful of great horses. All she needed was a long whip to crack. Mr Potter turned the wrong way and collided with the man in a dark suit, who let out a squawk of pain. "Sorry," said Mr Potter. "Trod on your toe. Oh, Lord—where am I supposed to—"

"To your *left*, Frank!" shouted Miss Duffy. "Now your arabesque!"

Trying to stand on one leg with the other foot extended behind him, Mr Potter did not realise that he was too close to Mr Pebblemarsh, who was pirouetting on tiptoe with his arms in the air. The raised foot caught him sharply behind the knees, causing Mr Pebblemarsh to fold up like a pen-knife. Collapsing, he crashed into Bert Beasley and the two of them fell noisily to the floor of the stage. Mr Pebblemarsh helped Bert to his feet and, with his arm round the huge man's shoulders, said, "We really must stop meeting like this."

"Stop, stop!" shouted Miss Duffy, waving her arms at the pianist. "*Thank* you, Mrs Gipsum! Somebody stop her," she added as Mrs Gipsum, her eyes on her music, played steadily on.

"You *must* get these turns right," said Miss Duffy sternly.

The men on the stage gazed at her hopelessly. Thev looked very dusty and hot.

Mrs Palgrave came in, followed by Wendy James, Helen Oldham and several other people, Danny's mother among them.

"How's it going?" enquired Mrs Palgrave cheerfully.

"Terrible," said Bert.

"They'll be all right," said Miss Duffy. "With practice. We'll try the other routine in a minute. The one that includes Danny."

"Ah, Sue!" said Mrs Palgrave, spotting her at the back of the hall. "You should be with the actors, dear, since you're prompting. No point in sitting there watching the dancers." She turned to the stage. "Jennifer, shall we swop over for a bit? If you could walk your dancers through the other routine in the common room, I'll use the stage so we can mark the moves in. Then we'll change back and you can go through it with the music."

"I don't know that I can stand the pace," said Mr Pebblemarsh pathetically. Nobody took any notice.

While the groups were changing over, Wendy James ran up the aisle to join Sue in the back row.

"Is Rachel here?" she asked anxiously.

"No," said Sue.

Wendy pushed a strand of her long, fair hair back from her face, looking at Sue nervously. "She must think I'm awful," she said.

Sue shrugged. "It's not your fault," she pointed out. "That's what understudies are for."

"I know," said Wendy. "But—well, I'd feel terrible if it was me it had happened to. Will you tell her something?"

"What?" asked Sue, who for some reason found the fair-haired, well-behaved Wendy rather irritating.

"Tell her, if Marcia comes back, or if she can persuade Mrs Palgrave to change her mind, I won't mind standing down for her. After all, it *is* her part."

"Oh." Sue felt rather ashamed of not liking Wendy. "Yes, of course I'll tell her. Thanks."

"Mind you," Wendy went on a little smugly. "I don't think *Helen* will stand down. She says she thinks she's better than Marcia anyway and she'll keep the part even if Marcia does come back."

Sue smiled inwardly at the thought of little Helen Oldham standing up to Marcia about anything. Wendy looked at her rather uncertainly and said, "I'd better go. Mrs Palgrave will be wanting me. You will tell Rachel, won't you?"

"Yes," said Sue. "I'll tell her." And thanks for nothing, she thought, as Wendy's prim little figure made its way back to the stage. Wendy could afford to sound magnanimous. She thought her part was perfectly safe.

The next hour went quickly. Mrs Palgrave and Miss Duffy made their groups work so hard that they almost forgot that the pantomime was fun and started to regard it with professional interest. At last everyone met in the Drama hall, where Jennifer Duffy wanted to rehearse her dancers with the music.

"Actors all sit down," said Mrs Palgrave, shooing them off the stage. "You've done well this morning—now you can relax and have a laugh."

"Laugh at my wonderful dancers?" said Miss Duffy indignantly. "You must be joking, Norah! Now," she went on for the benefit of the actors. "This dance is where Buttons has found the single glass slipper left behind by Cinders after the Ball. Not realising it's anything special, he thinks he's supposed to take it down to the kitchen with all the other shoes, to be cleaned. But of course, he can't find the other one. So this is a 'hunt the slipper' dance, with the men bending and stretching as they hunt high and low, and Danny taking the opportunity to get in the way and generally send things up. OK, Phyllis!"

Mrs Gipsum rattled out some jazzy music and the dancers plunged gamely into their routine. Danny looked even smaller than usual as he scurried about the stage, and Sue could see that, despite a bit of turning the wrong way and uncertainty, the dance would be very effective and very funny. They went through it twice, and at the end of the second performance there was a sudden sound of hearty handclapping. "Bravo!" shouted a voice from the door. "Marvellous!"

All heads turned.

Harry Mudd stood in the doorway, smiling genially. He advanced. "Just thought I'd look in and see how it's going," he said. "Marcia tells me neither of us are needed this morning."

An uneasy glance went round.

"It's a great little show," said Harry. He was wearing a loudly-checked Canadian lumberjacket with the collar turned up, and walked with his hands thrust confidently into his pockets. "Great," he repeated. "And a wonderful chance for my lucky daughter." He shook Mrs Palgrave's hand warmly, still smiling. "I really appreciate the way you've taken her to your hearts."

Mrs Palgrave's voice was quiet but it had a good carrying quality, and in the hush which had fallen in the hall, every word was clearly audible. "Mr Mudd," she said, her hand still in Harry's, "there seems to have been a misunderstanding somewhere. Marcia's absence for so many days, and the lack of response to notes from the school—"

"Absence?" Harry stopped smiling and released Mrs Palgrave's hand. "What do you mean, absence?"

"The last time any of us saw Marcia," said Mrs Palgrave steadily, "was on the night of the Hallowe'en festival."

Harry looked stricken. "What are you telling me?" he said huskily. "That my daughter has been playing truant? *Lying* to me?"

Miss Duffy jumped to her feet, gathering her wits a little belatedly, and called, "Dancers this way!" Glad to be released from the embarrassing scene, the fathers followed her back to the sixth form common room, but their departure was quiet and Mrs Palgrave's voice could still be heard. "I am sorry, Mr Mudd," she said. "But as we could get no assurance that Marcia would be returning to school, we have had to replace her as the Prince. It was holding up all the rehearsals, you see."

Harry turned and made for the door, walking in a kind of rapid shamble as if he hardly knew where he was going. Only when he reached it did he look back, and then he shouted, "You'll regret this! Most places they never give you a chance, but you've gone one better, haven't you? Gave her a chance then took it away again. If that's not the way to break anyone's heart, I don't know what is. And as for these kids—they're a load of little monsters. Steal her shoes, send her to the wrong classrooms, shut her up in a dark cupboard—I hope they're pleased with themselves!" The door swung to behind him as he went out and then opened again as his head reappeared. Danny stifled a nervous giggle. "And you'd better find someone else to play your Stepmother," Harry added. "Because I'm *finished*." And this time he went out and did not come back.

"Oh, dear," said Mrs Palgrave. "This pantomime seems to be absolutely fated." Then she smiled bravely. "Never mind! The show must go on! See you Monday, everyone." But Sue noticed that as she gathered up her scripts, Mrs Palgrave's hands shook a little.

The assembled people began to move out. Sue's father came in through the door and looked round the hall until he spotted his daughter. "Oh, there you are," he said. "Is there a maniac loose in this school?"

"Why?" asked Sue blankly.

"Because," said her father, "on my way into the car park I was forced off the drive by an oncoming car driven by some utter lunatic. He must have been doing sixty or more."

"What sort of car was it?" asked Sue. But she knew the answer before it came, and joined in with her father as they said together—"It was a Rolls Royce."

CHAPTER 11

A Cup of Tea

Rachel was in a much better temper on Monday. Approaching the group of people waiting for the school bus at Shop Corner in Tavenham, she waved cheerfully. "Hello!" she called. "I've had a lovely weekend!"

"Oh, good," said Matt a little warily.

"Yes, I went to Miss Pettit's, and when I came back Auntie Miriam and Uncle Peter said would I like to go to London with them, just for the weekend, and come back on the train on Sunday night! I think they realised I was feeling a bit fed up."

"I wouldn't be surprised," said Sue.

"Anyway," Rachel went on, ignoring the sardonic edge to Sue's remark, "that's what I did. And we went to see 'Ring Round the Moon' on Saturday night. It was *brilliant*, Sue. Honestly—"

"Did Sue tell you about Mr Mudd?" asked Danny, coming up to join them.

"Harry Mudd? No—why, what happened?"

"He found out Marcia hadn't been at school." Danny recounted Saturday morning's episode. "Fancy her being away all that time and him not knowing! He must have felt an awful twit."

"He nearly ran into my dad's car coming out," added Sue. "Dad said he was driving like a maniac. He had to go on to the grass to avoid him."

"Great stuff!" said Rachel, interested. "So what's going to happen about the Stepmother?"

"I don't know," said Danny. "But Mr Mudd won't do it. He was ever so cross."

The bus arrived, and they all climbed in, still talking. Rachel sat down beside Sue, but continued her conversation with Danny, leaning across the gangway so that she could hear what he said above the noise of the engine.

"We'll have to ask Ollie again," she said. "He'd make a super Stepmother."

"He won't," said Matt. "And he'll be cross if we go on pestering him."

"Mrs Palgrave will get him to do it," said Rachel confidently. "She can get people to do *anything*." She hugged herself, suddenly grinning with delight. "Isn't it all *interesting*!" she said.

When Mr Potter had finished calling the register, Rachel went up to his desk, looking earnest. "Sir," she said. "Can I ask you something?"

"Of course," said Mr Potter.

"Well—I feel a bit yukky about Marcia. I mean, we *did* tease her, and now Danny's told me what Mr Mudd said on Saturday it really does seem to be all my fault."

Mr Potter looked at her a little suspiciously.

"So I thought I ought to go round to her house and say I'm sorry," Rachel went on. "But the thing is, she probably won't want to talk to me."

"Possibly not," agreed Mr Potter. He was clearly still rather cross with Rachel.

"So I wondered—do you think I could take her some books? I mean, she is missing all the work, and she must be getting awfully bored with nothing to do all day. If I had something to *give* her, you see, it would make it much easier to start talking."

"M'm." Mr Potter thought about it, looking at Rachel. She gazed back with anxious concern, her face betraying no trace of amusement or malice. Mr Potter made up his mind. He sat back in his chair and said, "Yes, Rachel, I think that's a good idea. Somebody's got to do something. The social workers try their best, but there are times when the very fact of *being* social workers is against them, if you see what I mean."

"Yes, I do," said Rachel. "What should I take? Her Eng lish books, do you think?"

"Leave it to me," said Mr Potter. "I'll ask round the staff room at break, and see if anyone else wants to suggest anything, and I'll set her something to do. Nothing heavy. Something she might enjoy. When were you thinking of going?"

"I might go this evening, after school," said Rachel. "I can get the bus home from Flaxton. It *is* Prospect Row, isn't it?" she added innocently.

"That's right," agreed Mr Potter. "I'll look up the number for you." He smiled at Rachel. "It's nice to see people acting responsibly again," he said. "I've been very worried about you lot for the last few days."

"We're all right, really," Rachel assured him, beaming. She sat down beside Sue, looking very pleased with herself.

Matt leaned across and whispered, "What are you up to?"

"Nothing!" protested Rachel innocently.

"Come off it!" said Matt. If Rachel turned up at Prospect Row, Marcia would at once assume that it was because he had repeated their conversation in the café.

Rachel sighed gustily. "Why do you think?" she said. Mr Potter was burrowing about in his desk drawer and the conversation had become general. "Quite honestly, Matt, I want my part back. I don't care why Marcia said she lived in a country mansion, or what her father does, or anything else. For all I know they may be a pair of raving nutters. But I'm sick of her mucking everything up because she's got the sulks, and I'm going to see if I can talk her out of them. *Nicely*!" she added as Matt opened his mouth to protest.

The bell went for the first lesson, but as it was English with Mr Potter, they stayed in the same room. In the general bustle of getting out books, Matt tried to imagine a conversation between Rachel and Marcia. It seemed very likely, he thought, to do more harm than good. He put his English books on his desk slowly, thinking hard. There was only one thing to do. He would have to go to Prospect Row as well.

The last lesson that afternoon was Drama with Mrs Palgrave.

"Naturally enough," she told them, "we are all thinking about the pantomime at the moment. Now, pantomimes, as you know, are based on fairy stories, and fairy stories are about real life with a dash of magic thrown in. What I want you to do is, divide yourselves into groups of six or seven, and work out a little scene where something totally unexpected happens to someone in the middle of their ordinary life."

"Don't get it," said John Beasley.

"Think of Cinderella," explained Mrs Palgrave, "sitting there in her kitchen, wearing grubby old clothes and wishing she could go to the Ball. Then—bingo! In comes the Fairy Godmother and life is transformed into something different. I want you to think of a modern equivalent. It could be someone working at a factory bench, perhaps, or someone at a shop checkout or an office—just the ordinary, routine, boring old day—"

"Like school?" suggested Stephen, grinning.

"School, yes, that would do," agreed Mrs Palgrave, not rising to the bait. "But the thing is to bring in some magical, amazing person who transforms everything. You can have ten minutes or so to work it out, then we'll take it in turns for each group to act their improvised scene. Can you sort out your own groups or do you want me to do it?"

"We'll do it," said Danny. "Mrs Palgrave," he added. "Who's going to play the Stepmother in the pantomine now Mr Mudd won't?"

"I don't know," said Mrs Palgrave, looking worried. "All the people who might have done it are cast as someone else now. Why?"

"We thought Ollie Withett might be good," said Danny.

"Ollie," said Mrs Palgrave. "Yes, I never thought of him. Those great long arms—yes, he'd be marvellous. Thanks, Danny."

The improvisations turned out to be very funny. Bill North's group tried to do a sketch about a combine harvester which sprouted wings and flew to America, but as nobody could see the imaginary machine it was difficult to understand what was going on. Another group did a scene in a factory where the Fairy shop steward organised an impromptu disco, and a third had a queue of people waiting to pay for their goods in a supermarket joining up into a conga line and dancing their way round the shelves.

Rachel's group staged a poignant drama about a girl who was rescued from the boredom of school routine by the advent of a Drama production in which she, playing the leading role, was discovered by a visiting impresario. A second scene showed her triumphant stardom, but in the third scene she was back in the classroom, knowing that her success had been nothing but a daydream, and being scolded by the teacher (Danny doing his Mr Watts impression) for inattention.

Everyone laughed and clapped, and Rachel, bowing with the other members of her group, shot a glance at Mrs Palgrave, who shook her head, smiling. "Point taken, Rachel!" she said. "I know the pantomine has been a terrible disappointment to you, but every aspiring actress has her setbacks, you know. It's a tough profession and for every one who makes it, there are dozens who don't." She shrugged cheerfully. "I didn't, for instance. That's why I'm here. Now!" she added at once, turning to the others. "Collect up your things. The bell will go at any minute and when it does, go out quietly, please. See you next week."

The bell shrilled. With calls of "'Bye, miss!" they all went out.

"I never thought of it like that," said Sue.

"What?" asked Rachel.

"That teachers might have wanted to do something else. Do you think lots of them go into teaching as a sort of second best?"

"I don't know," said Rachel. "With things like music or drama I suppose they do. If your subject is English, there's nothing you can do *except* teach it, is there?"

"You could write," Matt pointed out. "Be on a newspaper or something."

"I suppose you could," agreed Rachel. "If you could spell well enough. Why *do* teachers teach, then?"

"Perhaps they like it," suggested Danny. "Long holidays."

"Lousy pay, though," said Rachel. "*I'm* not going to be a teacher."

"Nobody would have you," said Stephen. "And you're not going to get on the bus, either, if you don't hurry up."

"I'm not going on the bus tonight," said Rachel.

"Neither am I," said Matt.

Danny looked surprised. "Why not?" he asked.

"Got another dentist appointment," Matt lied. "Half-past four."

"You are a twit," said Stephen. "Fancy having an appointment outside school time!"

Matt blushed, aware that Danny was looking at him suspiciously. "Yes, well—better be off," he said, trying to sound casual. "See you tomorrow."

Danny was about to say something else, but Matt gave him a ghost of a wink and his small friend dutifully got on the bus with the others.

"Shall I go round to your house and tell your mother you'll be late, Rachel?" called Sue.

"No, I told her this morning," said Rachel.

"You mean, you'd planned to go anyway?" asked Matt. "Before we heard about what Harry Mudd said on Saturday morning?"

"Oh, yes," said Rachel carelessly. "I'd been rehearsing my little speech to Mr Potter all weekend. Good, wasn't it?"

"Oh marvellous," said Matt with foreboding.

Prospect Row led nowhere. It was a ridiculously wide road only a few hundred metres long, with houses on one side of it. A field came up to the ragged hedge on the other side, and the road ended in a weedy roundabout with the beginnings of two further roads leading off from it. These, however, came to an end in a few metres, and a couple of strands of barbed wire divided them from the ploughed earth.

Matt surveyed it grimly as he stood hidden from sight in a small bus shelter at the top of the road, waiting for Rachel. He had come straight here while Rachel was seeing Mr Potter about books for Marcia. He was glad that Prospect Row was only accessible from one end; Rachel would have to come this way in order to get to Marcia's house. He was bound to see her.

Matt stared across the road, envisaging Rachel walking with her quick stride along the far pavement. He was completely taken by surprise when she passed the bus shelter within a few centimetres of him. "Hi!" he shouted inanely.

Rachel jumped. She glanced crossly over her shoulder, then stopped. "Matt! What are you doing here?"

"I've got to tell you something,' said Matt—and instantly regretted it. He had been mentally trying out all sorts of ways of telling Rachel why he was here, but he hadn't meant to say exactly those words.

"What?" asked Rachel. "And why here?"

"Well—" Matt hesitated. If he told Rachel about his meeting with Marcia she would be bubbling over with it when they went to the house. Marcia would know at once that he had broken his word—and it would make things much worse.

"I'm coming with you," he said.

"To see Marcia? Why?"

"I just—want to," said Matt. He knew it must sound stupid.

Rachel stared at him. "Oh," she said, in a tone half-piqued and half-relieved. "Well—I don't see why. But you can come if you like."

They set off down Prospect Row.

"What made you decide to come?" asked Rachel.

"Don't know, really," said Matt, trying to sound offhand. "Just thought I would."

Rachel laughed. "Aren't you funny!" she said. "Fancy deciding at the last minute like that. Still—it's quite nice to have someone else along. I don't know what sort of mood she'll be in."

"Never do with her, do you?" said Matt casually. He glanced round at the bleak outlook. "Why on earth did they call it Prospect Row? I thought a prospect meant a promise of something nice. This place is a dump."

"It was going to be a big housing estate," Rachel told him. "The Post Office were planning to move a lot of people down here to work at a new place in Flaxton, and then it all fell through. The Council had started to build these houses but they stopped because there weren't going to be as many people as they thought. That's what my dad said, anyway."

"It's awful," said Matt. "It looks as if everyone's forgotten about it."

Dustbins stood just inside the gate in most of the overgrown gardens, and a rusted tricycle leaned against a doorstep amid a clutter of empty milk bottles, as if nobody came to the house anymore.

"Seventeen—eighteen—nineteen. That's the Mudds'," said Rachel. "The one with the clipped hedge."

"It's much neater than the others, isn't it?" said Matt. "Someone's making a big effort to tidy it up."

"Perhaps Mr Mudd likes gardening," said Rachel.

They opened the gate and went in. The grass had been cut and someone had been weeding the unkempt borders. Rachel rang the bell.

A thin, blonde woman of about thirty opened the door a few centimetres. She wore jeans and a man's shirt with the sleeves rolled up. "Yes?" she said.

"Is Marcia in?" asked Rachel.

"No," said the woman. "No, she's not." She atempted to shut the door.

"Do you know when she'll be back?" asked Rachel quickly. "We're her friends from school, you see. We've brought her some books."

"You could leave them here, I suppose," said the woman grudgingly.

"Oh, I don't think we'd better do that," said Rachel. "There's things to explain, you see. Mr Potter asked us."

"Oh, did he. Well, you'll have to come back another time," said the woman. The door began to close again.

"Just a minute," said Matt suddenly. "Are you Doreen?"

Rachel glanced at him in astonishment, and the woman at the door looked almost equally surprised. "Yes, that's me," she said. "How do you know?"

"Marcia told me," said Matt.

"Did she? Goodness—I didn't think she had any friends at school," said Doreen. "Not to *talk* to. From what she said, I thought they were a snooty lot. What's your name, love?"

"Matt Aiken. Honestly, we would like to see her," said Matt earnestly. "I know things haven't been too good at school, but—where's she gone, do you know? Perhaps we could meet her somewhere."

Doreen looked at Matt's round, snub-nosed face and suddenly smiled. "Matter of fact," she said confidingly, "she's up in her room. Harry said she wasn't to go out, and she said she didn't want to see anyone ever again—it's been a right old weekend with the pair of them, I can tell you." She stood back from the door. "Come on in." She closed the door behind Rachel and Matt and led the way upstairs. The house smelt of new paint.

Doreen knocked on a bedroom door.

"Go away," said Marcia from inside.

"Marcia, love, it's some friends from school to see you," said Doreen loudly. "Are you going to let them in?"

"I haven't *got* any friends!" shouted Marcia.

Doreen looked at Matt and shrugged.

Matt knocked boldly at the door and said, "Marcia! It's me, Matt. The one that looks like a Fred."

There was silence, then they heard the door being unlocked from inside. They waited for a moment, then Doreen pushed it open and stood back for them to go in. "I'll make some tea," she said.

Marcia was sitting on her bed, hands thrust into her jeans pockets, bare feet straddled on the bedside mat. She looked up as Matt came in, then, when she saw Rachel behind him, jumped to her feet.

"What d'you bring *her* here for?" she demanded furiously. "I told you, didn't I—"

"Nobody brings me anywhere," said Rachel firmly. Matter of fact, I brought Matt."

"Well, you can take him away again," said Marcia. "This is my house, innit. And I don't want to see nobody."

"We brought some books—" began Rachel.

Marcia laughed shortly. "You know what you can do with those, don't you," she said. "Now shove off, both of you."

She sat down on her bed again, scowling. Above her, the over-life-size portraits of pop stars sang silently on the walls.

Matt felt deeply embarrassed. It had been a stupid idea to come. He turned towards the door.

"Wait a minute," Rachel said to him. "What's been going on? How did you know Doreen's name?"

Matt blushed. That's done it, he thought. Now I'll have to tell her everything.

Marcia looked up at both of them. "Don't she know?" she asked, indicating Rachel with her thumb.

"Of course not," said Matt, his face pink and obstinate.

Marcia suddenly laughed. "Well, good old Fred," she said. "So you didn't tell her, after all." Then she shrugged, her momentary amusement gone. "No point in keeping it quiet now, is there?" she said. "I'm not going back to that place no more, so it don't matter if they all know. Have a good laugh." She nodded at Matt. "Go on—tell her."

Unwillingly, Matt explained how he had met Marcia in the café, and what she told him about Harry and his attempt to give his family the status he felt they deserved.

"There you are," said Marcia to Rachel when Matt had finished. "You wanted to know all about me, didn't you? Well, now you do. And you can go back to school and have a good time telling all the others. Oh, and the Rolls is borrowed. Fred left that bit out. Dad's got a Ford van. Go on, then," she added defiantly as Rachel said nothing. "Laugh!"

Rachel shook her head. She had her airline bag in one hand and the armful of books she had brought for Marcia in the other. "I think it's lovely," she said with an attempted smile that turned into a sob. "And I'm so sorry ." Then she was in floods of tears. She put her bag down on the floor and groped in her pocket for a handkerchief. Matt went and looked out of the window. What on earth was Rachel crying about? She usually seemed so tough and determined.

"Don't be daft," said Marcia uncomfortably. "I mean, there's nothing for *you* to cry about." She took a tissue out of the box beside her bed and gave it to Rachel.

"If you'd—" gulped Rachel after some minutes—"if you'd only *said*."

Matt turned away from the window. "I told you she was all right really," he said to Marcia.

Marcia nodded. They both watched Rachel crying and then Marcia said in a kind of wail, "Oh, do stop it—you'll start me off!" Tears welled in her eyes, spilled over and made two dark rivulets down her cheeks. "Blooming mascara," she muttered, blotting her face crossly with a tissue. "Supposed to be runproof. Never is." Matt, glancing from one weeping girl to the other, began to grin. He felt immensely relieved, but this really was pretty ridiculous. They both looked at him, sniffing, and he tried to suppress a laugh, unsuccessfully.

Rachel gave a watery smile, blew her nose and turned to Marcia with a slight gesture of the hands which somehow combined apology with an offer of friendship. "Oh, well," said Marcia, tacitly accepting it. "What the heck."

There was a tap at the door and Doreen entered, elbow first, with a tray of tea. "I'm ever so glad you two have come," she said, putting the tray down on the dressing table. "When Harry said that about the school not being what he thought it was, I thought, oh no, here we go again. Every school Marcia's been at, he says there's been trouble. Put it down to these fuddy-duddy old faggots they have teaching. He was that thrilled to find one that seemed a bit different—then when things went wrong it was that much more of a disappointment, I suppose." She noticed that Rachel and Marcia had been crying and paused uncertainly. "You all right, love?" she asked Marcia.

Marcia looked up at her, and a grin spread across her streaked face. "Yeah," she said. "I'm all right."

"Do you think she *will* come to school tomorrow?" asked Rachel. They were walking back along Prospect Row towards the bus stop in Windsor Avenue. It was dark now and raining slightly. A group of boys on the other side of the road kicked an empty Coke tin along before them with a hollow clattering noise.

"I don't know," said Matt. "I wouldn't blame her if she didn't."

They walked in silence for some way. The sound of the tin stopped as one of the boys finally kicked it into the field. Matt glanced at Rachel uneasily. She seemed depressed.

"Don't give up hope," he said encouragingly. "Marcia

said she *might* come back, and if she does, you'll get your pantomine part back again, won't you?"

"Oh, shut up!" said Rachel angrily.

"Why?" persisted Matt. "That's what you want, isn't it?"

"Yes, but—oh, can't you see? I never thought of Marcia as a person at all. She was just something getting in my way, and I feel awful about it. I'd never have been like that if I'd known."

"But you didn't know," Matt pointed out.

"Why couldn't I have guessed?" Rachel lamented.

"You're being silly," said Matt firmly. "I don't know why you're so up in the air. Everything's either marvellous or it's terrible. And it really isn't like that."

"It seems like that to me," said Rachel.

Matt thought about the scene which had just taken place and decided that Rachel was probably just acting. The tears had done the trick all right—Marcia had become a completely different person. But he couldn't help remembering that Rachel's innocent-sounding conversation with Mr Potter that morning had been carefully rehearsed. She had said so, and laughed about it. "It must be great, being able to act," he said.

"What d'you mean?" asked Rachel.

"Well—seeming all upset when you were talking to Marcia. It certainly worked. She believed every word."

"Matthew Aiken, you utter *beast*!" wailed Rachel. "I *did* mean it. Of *course* I did!" And, to Matt's alarm, her eyes filled with tears again. He was immensely relieved to see the bus come round the corner.

CHAPTER 12

The End of the Line

Marcia came to school the next morning, on the bus from Flaxton. She stalked across the bus park amid whistles and cat calls from the boys, dangling her orange bag in one hand, the other thrust into the pocket of a vastly oversized and rather grubby donkey jacket. She still wore her high-heeled shoes but had exchanged her tight trousers for a black skirt with a slit up the side.

"Hello, Marcia!" said Mr Potter as he came into his room to find her sitting in her place beside Felicity. "Nice to see you back!"

Marcia nodded and said nothing, but moved the wad of gum she was chewing from one side of her mouth to the other.

"Er—we don't allow chewing gum, I'm afraid," said Mr Potter rather nervously.

"I'll bung it down the loo later," said Marcia casually. "Thanks for sending the books. I brought them back."

"Oh, good," said Mr Potter.

John Beasley looked aggrieved and said, "Make her put her gum in the basket. You would if it was me."

"John, will you kindly mind your own business," said Mr Potter angrily.

Marcia sighed. She got up, slouched between the desks to the wastepaper basket and deposited her chewing gum. "There," she said, returning. "Now you won't have no quarrels about it."

"Thank you," said Mr Potter.

The morning's History lesson passed without incident. Although Mrs Abbott glared at Marcia's pink-varnished fingernails with pursed lips, she made no comment.

"Bet they've all been told to be careful what they say to Marcia," Rachel whispered to Sue.

"Rachel Greenberg, be quiet at once!" snapped Mrs Abbott.

"Yes, miss," said Rachel.

At break, Rachel said to Marcia, "Are you coming for a walk round the field?"

"No," said Marcia. "Muddy, innit."

"Not really," said Matt, overhearing. "It didn't rain much last night."

"Don't like grass," said Marcia. "My heels sink in."

"We'll go on the paved bit, then," said Rachel. She got a tube of sweets out of her bag and offered Marcia one.

"Ta," said Marcia.

They sat down on a bench. Danny and Sue came to join them. "We were sitting here the first morning you arrived," said Danny. "Eating crisps."

"What did you say when you saw the Roller?" asked Marcia. "'Who's this coming, Lady Muck?'"

"Something like that," agreed Matt.

"What a laugh," said Marcia. She pushed her hands into her donkey-jacket pockets and stuck her legs out, balancing one foot on top of the other on its spiky heel.

"Is that your dad's jacket?" asked Sue, remembering Harry wearing something similar on that first day.

"Yeah. They've all got the idea I'm a welfare case, so I thought I'd look deprived," said Marcia. "Makes you look small if your clothes is too big. Good, innit?" She rolled her dark-circled eyes tragically.

"Don't you start!" said Sue. "Rachel's always doing things like that."

Rachel and Marcia exchanged a brief grin. There was still a little constraint between them, but Matt noticed with relief that each of them was being very careful not to say anything which might upset the other.

"What shall we do about the pantomime?" asked Rachel cautiously. "Do you still want to be in it?"

"Wouldn't mind," said Marcia.

"The thing is," Rachel went on, "Helen's taken over your part. And because she and I don't look right together, Wendy James has taken mine."

Marcia laughed shortly. "No wonder you wanted me back at school," she said without malice.

"Mrs Palgrave won't want to change things round again," said Danny. "Not unless she's sure you'll go on being here."

"Yeah," said Marcia. She stared at the line of trees which marked the edge of the field, screwing up her nose doubtfully. "Dunno," she said. "I'll have to think."

Sue felt Rachel stiffen with annoyance and said quickly, "You'll have to think pretty fast. I mean, there's a lot of people in the pantomime all depending on you."

"If you *don't* come back here," said Matt, changing the subject, "what will you do? Will the Council send you to another school?"

Marcia did not answer at once. Then she stopped looking at the trees and sighed. "Matter of fact," she said, "I *got* to stay here. End of the line, innit."

"What do you mean?" asked Sue.

"Dad says the Council will take him to court if I don't go to school," said Marcia. "And they'll probably put me back in care. That's why he was so mad when he found out I was skiving."

Nobody knew what to say.

"Thing is," Marcia went on, "you get used to not being at school. Once you get the idea you don't have to go, that's it. After that, you can't sit in a classroom with some silly old bag telling you off about things that don't matter. What do they know about it, anyway? They've had it easy—must have, or they wouldn't be teachers."

"I know what you mean," said Rachel. "They do rabbit on. Some of them are all right, though. I think the thing is to get what you want from it and try not to worry about the rest."

"Yeah," said Marcia bleakly. "S'pose so." The bell went and she made a face. "'Ere we go again." They all picked up their bags and wandered slowly back towards the building.

After an early lunch, Rachel and Sue, together with Marcia and Danny and several interested onlookers, went into the Drama hall. Ollie Withett, clutching a script and scowling with embarrassment, was on the stage with Wendy James as Cinders.

"Speak up, Wendy," exhorted Mrs Palgrave. "Stand with your shoulders back, so you can get more air into your lungs. No, not stiffly—try to feel your rib cage lift. A quick, *deep* breath is what you need."

Wendy's shoulders went up to her ears as she tried to obey this instruction. "I have been peeling potatoes for three hours, Stepmamma," she announced in a stangled scream.

"Oh no, dear—relax!" said Mrs Palgrave. "You look like a shirt that's been hung out in icy weather and frozen stiff."

Marcia gave a snort of laughter, and Mrs Palgrave turned and saw her. "Glad you're back," she said, "but don't interrupt. Go and sit down, you lot. Now, Wendy, practise taking deep breaths and holding them. Yes, offstage, in the wings. Ollie, let's try your bit again."

"Anyone—should—be—able to—peel—half a ton—of potatoes—in three hours," Ollie read laboriously.

"Yes. Now just *say* it, Ollie, without the script."

"Anyone can peel half a ton of spuds in three hours," mumbled Ollie. He frowned. "That's rubbish, Miss. They can't."

"Never mind. Now, Ollie, you're going to look simply wonderful in a long skirt and high heels, but you've got the same problem as Wendy. You must speak slowly and clearly, but sound natural."

Ollie looked hopeless.

"I'm sure you can do it," said Mrs Palgrave. "Let's go through the whole scene. Wendy!"

Wendy came on to the stage with her eyes watering. Mrs Palgrave looked at her doubtfully. "I hope you haven't been overdoing the breath-holding," she said. "Right. Ollie—from 'What have you been doing, girl'."

"What have you been doing girl," said Ollie tonelessly.

"I have been peeling potatoes for three hours, Stepmamma," screamed Wendy. She caught her breath and began to cough. Ollie, ignoring her, read stolidly on. "Any one—should—be—"

"Stop, stop!" shouted Mrs Palgrave. "Let her recover, Ollie, for goodness' sake. Oh, this pantomime is an absolute disaster."

Helen Oldham appeared from the wings and said, "I haven't had my dinner yet, Mrs Palgrave. Can I go?"

Mrs Palgrave, who was standing on the floor of the hall by the edge of the stage, flung her script down on the boards. "Yes, *go* and have your dinner!" she shouted. "All of you, go and stuff your faces with sausage and mash and I hope you enjoy it. What *is* the use?"

"Oh!" murmured Rachel, delighted. "Temperament!"

The Drama hall door opened and a figure in a boiler suit appeared. For a moment nobody realised who it was, then Marcia called; "Hello, Dad!"

"Oh, no," Mrs Palgrave muttered audibly. "This is all we need."

Harry Mudd walked across the hall to where Mrs Palgrave stood. "I had to come in and see the Head," he said, "about young Marcia. And I thought I best pop in. Just to say I didn't ought to have spoken to you the way I did. You're doing a good job, girl." He took Mrs Palgrave's hand in his own large one and shook it, then patted her on the shoulder in a fatherly way.

"I'm not," said Mrs Palgrave wretchedly. "It's a *terrible* job." She looked as if she was going to cry.

Ollie stared down at Harry. "Ere!" he said. "Are you the bloke that's supposed to be doing this?"

"I was," said Harry.

"Then you can have it, mister," said Ollie. He came to the edge of the stage and added, "Was it you driving Johnny Bennett's Rolls on Saturday?"

"Ollie—" began Mrs Palgrave warningly.

"I want to know," insisted Ollie.

Harry pushed his hands into his boiler-suit pockets. "Yes," he said. "That's me."

"Well, just mind where you drive it," said Ollie indignantly. You went so quick, you made another bloke turn off right over my grass—made two bloody great ruts in it."

"Sorry about that," said Harry. "I'll see you right for the extra work, mate. And I shan't be borrowing the Roller no more. Don't need it."

Helen Oldham, who had been staring down at Marcia, suddenly announced, "I'm not giving up my part just because *she's* come back. I don't care what anyone says."

"Whoops!" said Danny. "Mrs Palgrave won't like that."

Mrs Palgrave didn't like it at all. "You, Miss Oldham," she said coldly, "will do exactly as you are told."

"I've spent every single dinner hour in here," complained Helen, "mostly just hanging about—*and* Saturday mornings, and I don't see why I should be mucked about after all that. And I'm better then she is, anyway."

Danny gave a loud whistle of disapproval.

"Gone to her head," whispered Marcia to Rachel.

"OTT!" agreed Rachel.

Mrs Palgrave glared at Helen. "Right," she said. "That settles it. As from now, we return to the original cast."

Rachel impetuously flung her arms round Marcia, who said, "Get off!" but grinned as she said it. Helen burst into noisy tears and ran out of the hall. Wendy said, "Honestly, Mrs Palgrave, I'm quite glad. I can't seem to get my rib cage right." And, demure as ever, she followed Helen out.

Ollie jumped down from the stage and said, "I better get back to my grass."

"Thanks a lot, Ollie," said Mrs Palgrave. "I know you didn't want to do it, and it was very nice of you to try."

"'Sall right," said Ollie. "Glad you got the right bloke back." And he, too, went out.

Mrs Palgrave looked at Harry Mudd and gave a little gasp of dismay. "Oh, Lord!" she said. "I am an idiot!"

"Why?" asked Danny who, with the others, had left the seats in the hall to cluster round Mrs Palgrave.

"I've packed Ollie and the others off without asking you people if you'll do it," she said. "I know Rachel will, but what about you, Marcia? I can't stand the strain if you're going to be unreliable."

"I'll be here," said Marcia.

"You're sure?" queried Mrs Palgrave.

Marcia nodded. "Sure," she said.

Harry's old self-confidence had returned, and when Mrs Palgrave looked at him questioningly, he stuck his thumbs in the lapels of his boiler suit and said, "Have no fear—Harry's here!"

Mrs Palgrave glanced at the clock on the wall. "We've still got half an hour before the bell goes," she said. "How about going through this scene with Rachel and Mr Mudd?"

"Harry," corrected Harry. "Yes, that's all right. They won't be expecting me back at work until two."

Sue and Marcia sat down in the front row while Rachel and Harry went through the scene.

"They're much better than the other two!" whispered Sue.

Marcia nodded. "Yeah," she said.

They watched for another few minutes, then Sue said, "You know, I think you and Rachel are awfully alike in some ways."

Marcia grinned. Rachel was twisting her hands in an imaginery apron as she explained to Harry in her clearly audible voice why she had failed to peel half a ton of potatoes in three hours. "Looks a right welfare case, don't she?" she said. "You could be right, bun-face." She fished in her orange bag for a packet of chewing gum and offered a piece to Sue.

"Ta," said Sue.

When the scene ended, Mrs Palgrave stared into the auditorium and said, "Are you two *chewing*?"

"Yeah," said Marcia. "You don't mind, do you—really?"

Mrs Palgrave looked at her. "It's not the chewing I mind," she said. "It's parking the blasted stuff under the seats."

"We won't do that," said Sue.

"Promise!" agreed Marcia.

"You'd better not," said Mrs Palgrave with menace, and turned back to the stage.

Marcia grinned. "I like Mrs P," she said to Sue. "She's all right. And anyway, we got old Watts this afternoon. We'll stick it under *his* seats instead."

The rest of the term went past in no time. Marcia stayed at school because of the pantomime and soon became Rachel's inseparable friend. Mrs Abbott was heard to say that the combination of Rachel Greenberg and Marcia Mudd was enough to try the patience of a saint.

Although Matt still refused to have anything to do with acting, he found himself roped in as a ticket-seller, crossing off the seats as they were sold on large diagrams of the auditorium. His job was finished at least three weeks before the end of term, for the pantomime was sold out for every performance.

The final dress rehearsal, staged before an audience of pensioners from the local old people's homes, was a disaster. Roger Smart left the overhead working light on, so the black-out at the end of the Ball scene left the stage clearly lit, and Ollie Withett, working as a scene-shifter, was heard saying loudly, "I'm not shifting nothing with them lot looking." Mr Pebblemarsh put his pink-slippered foot through the scenery during the ballet and everyone forgot their lines. But the old people shrieked and cackled with laughter, and Mrs Palgrave said firmly, "Bad dress rehearsal—good first night. Everyone knows that."

"Yes, but does the audience know?" Rachel muttered darkly.

As it turned out the performances were a huge success. Rachel and Marcia got better and better as Cinders and the Prince, and one night there were such loud cheers after their duet, "Round About Midnight", that they had to do an encore. Mrs Gipsum, who had written the song, blushed with pleasure at the piano, and Mr Fox, playing a trombone in the orchestra, got up and shook her hand so enthusiastically that she lost a contact lens and the first violins spent the whole of the interval looking for it.

Matt helped Mr Pebblemarsh and Mrs Bath with the make-up, and did not see the performance from "in front" until the final night, when he had booked seats for himself and his mother. He joined her as the house lights were going down, his fingers still multicoloured with eyeliner and rouge.

"Hello!" she whispered. "What a lovely atmosphere, isn't it! Just like a real theatre!"

"Hope so!" Matt whispered back—and realised for the first time that he had become part of the pantomime, absolutely involved in its exciting, cranky, peculiar life. The curtain went up and he settled back to enjoy himself.

Harry Mudd, with a cushion from one of the staff room chairs stuffed down his bodice to produce an enormous bust, was scolding Cinders. "Gels these days," he squawked in a voice aimed at gentility but constantly lapsing into the common, "haven't got no refainment." His blue-rinsed wig slipped over one eye and he paused with an unhurried pursing of the lips to adjust it and tuck in an imaginary curl. The audience rocked with laughter, and Rachel as Cinders continued to gaze at Harry with a trembling lip which made him seem even funnier. Her own wig, long and wispy and faded brown, made her look completely different. "Aren't they good!" whispered Matt's mother.

Marcia made her entrance, slapping her hand on her thigh and demanding, "Where is my horse?" Felicity and Deb cantered in and leaned against the table, both crossing their hoofs. "Woops!" said Matt, seeing the table begin to slide. The horse staggered, tried to regain its balance, and fell flat on the boards with wild neighing. "Gosh!" said Matt in admiration. "Good old Deb! Fancy neighing as she fell! Mrs Palgrave *will* be pleased!"

"Wasn't it meant? asked his mother, laughing and clapping with everyone else. "I thought it looked like part of the act."

Mr Potter's pas de deux with Mr Pebblemarsh was hilarious. Mr Pebblemarsh, far the taller of the two, side-stepped daintily on to the stage with his long, bony arms held above his head. He was clad in a tight-fitting white bodice and frilly skirt, his huge feet crammed into outsize pink ballet shoes and a headdress of white feathers pinned insecurely on to his shaggy reddish-brown hair. His beard looked more bushy than ever as he tried with wildly bulging eyes to assume the poetic "look" demanded by Miss Duffy, standing with one hairy leg extended behind him. He gave a start of surprise as

Mr Potter, resplendent in floppy-sleeved blouse, tunic, tights and thick spectacles, leapt in and fell on his knees before him. The dance became more absurd as Mr Potter, gamely taking the classic "supporting role", tried to lift Mr Pebblemarsh's fourteen stone bulk. The huge, bearded ballerina shook the stage with every landing, and Mr Potter was soon perceptibly out of breath. The final effort to support Mr Pebblemarsh in a graceful nose-dive position proved too much for him and they both collapsed in a heap. They scrambled to their feet, casting nervous glances at the invisible Miss Duffy in the wings, and went through the rest of the dance at top speed in order to catch up with the music. Mrs Gipsum, having failed to notice that anything untoward had occurred, played steadily on, accompanied by a few giggling violins. The wind players were laughing too much to blow a note.

The curtain fell to rapturous applause. "Oh," gasped Matt's mother, wiping her eyes. "I've never seen anything so funny. Shall we get some coffee?"

"Actually," said Matt, "I said I'd give a hand with patching up the make-up in the interval. Coffee's in the sixth form common room. Oh, look, there's Stephen's parents. You know them, don't you?"

Seeing his mother safely taken care of, Matt went backstage. "We should have thought of the horse falling over before," Mrs Palgrave was saying regretfully. "We could have done it every night." Debbie and Felicity, rubbing their bruises, said in chorus, "*No, we couldn't!*"

"Oy," said Marcia, digging Matt in the ribs. "Come over here." Matt followed her to a corner of the dressing room, where Rachel was putting the finishing touches to her costume for the Ball scene. "Oh, Matt," she said. "We want you on the stage at the end, with Stephen and Ollie and all the others who helped backstage. We've got flowers for Mrs Palgrave and Miss Duffy and everyone, and Mr Hazzard's going to make a speech."

"I'm not going on the *stage*!" said Matt, alarmed.

"Yes, you are, Fred," said Marcia firmly. "Rude else, innit?" Her amazingly red hair, tumbling from under the hat with its ostrich feathers, for once looked absolutely right.

"But I'm in the audience tonight," said Matt. "My mother's here."

"Give her a treat, then," said Marcia. "She'll love seeing you on stage. All mums do. Doreen's here, too—in the middle of the third row. I keep trying not to look at her."

"You can stay in your seat until the end," Rachel assured him. "Slip out at the first curtain and come round backstage. You'll have plenty of time—there are bound to be two or three calls. Then you can join the rest of the company when Mr Hazzard makes his speech."

"Oh—all right, then," said Matt, resigned.

"Have courage!" said Marcia in her Prince Charming voice, and slapped him on the shoulder so encouragingly that she nearly knocked him flat.

Matt sat through the second half in a slight state of dread, although Danny's impersonation of Mr Watts brought the house down and his dance with Miss Duffy's men was so successful that they had to repeat it. Matt knew he didn't have to say anything or do anything, but the thought of being up there where everyone could see him was enough to make him nervous. When the curtain came down on the final tableau of the assembled cast, he made his way out of the hall and joined the others in the hot, sweaty, scented smell of the stage.

"Come on," said Roger Smart, clattering down the ladder from the lighting gallery, "all you stage hands—and where's Ollie?"

Matt shuffled on with the others, glad that Ollie's bulk more or less hid him from view. As speeches were made and flowers presented, he forgot his nervousness and edged into a position where he could see more easily what was going on.

"And now," Mr Hazzard was saying, "our leading ladies. First, the beautiful Prince Charming."

Marcia bowed, sweeping off her hat. Mr Pebblemarsh, still in his white tutu, strode on with a sheaf of carnations and gladioli and presented them to Marcia with a knock-kneed curtsey. Then, abandoning his efforts to behave like a dancer, he bent down and kissed her cheek. "You were smashing, kid," he said. When the applause died down he turned and added, "And now—Cinders!"

Amid renewed applause, it was Harry, his wig now hopelessly askew, who came forward to give Rachel her bouquet. He bowed and kissed her hand, and Rachel dropped a deep curtsey. Quietly, while the audience clapped, he said, "You were great, love. And thanks for everything."

Rachel blushed under her make-up. Rising, she said in her stage voice, "It's all been wonderful. Thank you." Then she stood on tiptoe and gave Harry a kiss.

"The Mayor!" called someone. "Make way for the Mayor!"

A corpulent man in a dark suit, resplendent in a gold chain, made his way to the centre of the stage and held up his hand. "Ladies and gentlemen," he began, "I am not going to make a long speech—"

"Hooray!" said Harry recklessly.

"—but I do want to say," the Mayor continued when the laughter died down, "that a school which can put on a show like this is a *happy* school." Several people groaned ironically, and the Mayor's red face turned a little redder. "It is a school where people get on easily," he persisted, "with no friction or quarelling. Where everyone understands everyone else."

"Except Mr Watts," muttered Danny. The entire company on the stage was convulsed with laughter, and the Mayor decided that his speech actually *would* be a short one. "So congratulations to all concerned," he ended. "Jolly well done!"

The curtain came down for the last time.

Rachel peeled off her wig. "No friction or quarelling!" she said, grinning. "He's got to be joking!"

"What a twit," said Marcia cheerfully. "He don't know nothing about it." She and Rachel went off to the dressing room, talking animatedly.

Matt stood on the empty stage, which seemed like a cosy, windowless room in its curtained privacy, and listened to the retreating babble of the audience as people filed out of the exit doors. Voices and laughter came from the backstage dressing rooms as the cast, still excited and wound-up, started to take off their make-up and change into their ordinary clothes. Danny wandered past, unbuttoning the row of brass buttons down his white tunic.

"You were very good," said Matt.

"Thanks!" said Danny, grinning. And he went on into the dressing room. Matt gave a small, happy sigh. He wouldn't have missed this pantomime for anything.

MILL GREEN

School Series

by Alison Prince

You can read more about Matt, Danny, Rachel and Sue — and the rest of the First Form mob — in their other exciting Armada adventure. Make sure you don't miss it.

Mill Green on Fire

When someone starts fires in the school and blames Ollie, the caretaker, Matt is determined to catch the real culprit. But his brilliant plan to catch the firebug goes horribly wrong . . .

More stories about Mill Green will be published in Armada.